TRAVELLING
RESERVE

TRAVELLING RESERVE

IAN WOOLDRIDGE

Collins
St James's Place, London
1982

William Collins Sons and Co Ltd
London · Glasgow · Sydney · Auckland
Toronto · Johannesburg

British Cataloguing in Publication Data
Wooldridge, Ian
Travelling reserve
1. Wooldridge, Ian 2. Journalists, British
– Biography
I. Title
070'.92'4 PN5123.W/

ISBN 0 00 216660 7

First published in Great Britain 1982

Made by Lennard Books
The Old School
Wheathampstead
Herts AL4 8AN

Editor Michael Leitch
Designed by David Pocknell's Company Ltd
Production Reynolds Clark Associates Ltd
Printed and bound in Spain by
TONSA, San Sebastian
Dep. Legal SS 418/1982

Contents

Chapter One

HOW TO ADDRESS A TYPEWRITER

A random survey of the famous bars along Fleet Street between noon and closing time any day except Saturday would do little to dispel an ugly rumour. It is that if a career in sportswriting demanded academic qualifications beyond an accidental O-level in metalwork, most British newspapers would end with four blank pages.

British sportswriters, almost to a man, live by the Hemingway creed that movement should never be confused with action. Thus the archetypal sportswriter's working day tends to start with field research over several glasses of lunch in either El Vino's or Scribes' Cellar and end in heated debate about Geoffrey Boycott's patriotism in the Press Club some fourteen hours later.

This, of course, is provided you are not in Australia with England's cricketers or New York for a big fight. In that case the same argument will be

"WHERE THE HELL'S WOOLDRIDGE? IT'SH HISH ROUND!"

going on in either the Sydney Press Club or Costello's Bar on East 44th Street. Sportswriters are frequently uncomfortable in the presence of outsiders, particularly those with views about sport.

From time to time the sportswriter is required to address a typewriter. This is mostly to fill out expenses forms itemizing the horrendous amounts of largesse that have to be invested in restaurants and night clubs these days in order to extract from sportsmen, referees, mistresses, politicians and former Sports Council employees the kind of information that makes a sports page worth reading.

The university has yet to be founded which offers graduate courses in these matters. Only in America is it possible for earnest young men to major in journalism, whatever that means. This explains why much American sportswriting, with a few formidable exceptions, reads as though it has been computed in a word-processing machine.

One of the exceptions was Red Smith, of the *New York Times*, who was once asked whether sportswriting was a difficult trade. 'There's nothing to it,' Mr Smith replied. 'You merely sit there at a typewriter and think until the blood seeps out of the pores on your forehead.' I once saw him seeping blood at the end of a golf tournament in Ireland. His chair was ankle-deep in crushed balls of paper. These were the introductory paragraphs he had fought with and discarded before hitting on one that would grab the reader by the throat and pin him down for the next 1,200 words.

Work, however, is the unspoken area of a business whose main credentials are swift two-finger typing, knowing how coin-telephones operate in Kiev, having the wisdom to leave semi-colons to those who believe they know how to use them, and a metabolism that can cope with jet-lag, Indian sanitation, Australian hospitality, and hangovers. Anyone with the remotest understanding of what happens inside fuse boxes or internal combustion engines is unlikely ever to make a sportswriter. Anyone who prefers to sit down and write for three hours and then pay someone *else* to paint the bathroom is at least morally equipped for the struggle.

Most English sportswriters started out desperately wanting to play for England at anything, failed, and then pestered their way on to local weekly newspapers with names like *The Bugle* or *Sentinel*. Mine, in Hampshire, was called the *New Milton Advertiser* and was run by a proprietor-editor who had a roll-top desk, candlestick telephone and, while writing powerful leader columns, hawked and spat into the waste-paper basket at seven-minute intervals between November and March. He was a benevolent bully, a brilliant journalist and was convinced that Lenin had personally founded the National Union of Journalists. Most of the apprentice reporters he employed on Dickensian salaries were in Fleet Street inside four years.

The editorial offices were a prefabricated bungalow heated by paraffin stoves that made noises like irritated cobras. The paper did not run to a specialist sportswriter. It employed young men with acne and bicycles who were expected to report local cricket, football and darts on Saturdays as a relaxation after a week at magistrates' courts, council meetings, inquests, weddings and flower shows.

Its big circulation-booster, however, was funerals. Funerals attracted mourners. Mourners who got their names into the *Advertiser* always bought one copy and frequently three.

My first assignment in journalism, apart from scuttling off to fetch twenty Senior Service for the chief reporter, was the funeral of Charles Browning, coal merchant and wealthy pillar of rectitude of the parish, God rest his soul.

Charles Browning has lain at peace these past thirty years in a lovely New Forest churchyard but getting him there was a less tranquil business

altogether. No-one had advised me that the trick was to get to the church, which was a mile from the graveside, an hour before the kick-off to collect the names, full initials and, in some cases, former service ranks plus decorations of those attending – on their way *in*. They just gave you a spiral-bound notebook and a 4B pencil and assumed everything would be OK.

It was. But not before a fledgling reporter had blocked the church doorway to scribble the names, full initials, former service ranks and decorations of the mourners – on their way *out*. None passed unrecorded but the half-hour of strain on the sagging pallbearers waiting to slide the coffin of the coal-tycoon into the hatch-back hearse for his last terrestrial journey was not quickly forgotten.

It was nothing to do with sport, but it was incomparable training for hijacking important witnesses, on their way out after disciplinary hearings against naughty footballers, and real little anarchists like John McEnroe, many years later. Foot-in-the-door techniques now meet with the disapproval of the Press Council but by a fortuitous

oversight the Press Council has no sportswriters sitting on it.

No reporter will ever work harder than during his seven-day, 6,000-word week on a highly disciplined local rag. You learn about fire engines, how rates are levied, suicides, head-on car collisions, what corpses look like, how to cheat in husbanding prize-winning root vegetables, perjury, how the scoring works at lawn bowls and that local sports club officials are frequently close personal relatives of Adolf Hitler.

My first really big sports assignment, after Les Tomkin's nine-for-21 for New Milton against Brockenhurst, came out of the blue. The telephone rang and a lady said: 'I'm here on vacation from America. Perhaps you'd like to interview me. Why not come to dinner?' By the grace of a mis-spent school career reading piles of sports magazines, I recognized the name. This was the big one.

The bus fare was ten pence to the outskirts of a neighbouring town. Bathed, Brylcreemed, aftershaved and as sophisticated as a seventeen-year-old reporter can be in a Harris tweed sports jacket, blue trousers and brown crepe-soled shoes, I rang the door bell and was greeted by a lady with much lipstick and a plunging neckline. She was not unknown in the world of motor-racing and was then forty-one.

After dinner, at her suggestion, we moved to the greater comfort of a deep floral loose-covered settee to examine a sheaf of American newspaper clippings extolling her sporting achievements. They made no mention of her other predilections which included almost instantaneous assaults on the zip-flies of petrified young local newspaper reporters. What followed was hardly one of the most protracted in-depth interviews in the history of sports journalism but it did, as they say, sort of get one started.

Chapter Two

THIS THING CALLED SPORT

My youthful ambition to bat second wicket down for England in the wake of Denis Compton was obliterated in the time it took Tom Dean to bowl four balls on the County Ground, Southampton. Dean bowled leg-breaks and googlies for Hampshire just after the war and it must have grieved him to squander them on a plump little left-hander who missed the first three and had his off-stump flattened by the fourth. Thus at a stroke, or more accurately no stroke at all, ended my career with the Hampshire Schoolboys' team and with it all dreams of a dazzling career in Test cricket. My hair started falling out soon after that so I could never have usurped Denis Compton's place in the Brylcreem advertisements anyway.

The incident raises a mild moral issue: whether a sportswriter who arbitrarily promotes himself to the pulpit of critic is entitled to criticize a sportsman whose game he

can't play. Obviously I believe he is, but, for all that, I am amazed I haven't been hit for some of the things I have written about sportsmen. I am even more astonished that I know of only one fracas between player and sportswriter. Returning from England's less-than-successful cricket tour of West Indies in 1981 Ian Botham read a less-than-flattering appraisal of his captaincy by Henry Blofeld in a copy of *The Guardian* that someone less-than-tactfully had left in the plane. There followed, during a re-fuelling stop at Bermuda, a less-than-dignified confrontation between subject and author.

The irony was that Blofeld is one of the very few newspapermen who might actually have played for England had he not stepped off a pavement at an inopportune moment. After batting beautifully for Eton, Cambridge and Norfolk he walked straight under a bus.

Despite this he was asked on the 1964 tour of India to stand by to field for England in a Test Match during one of those perennial crises when half the team are groaning with the intestinal disorders that come from eating almost anything other than hard-boiled eggs or bananas. Unfortunately England bravely staggered on, Blofeld's call never came and I was thus deprived of any motive for writing a delicious item of gossip concerning Ian Fleming's close friendship with Henry's family. When Fleming started writing the James Bond thrillers that were to take the publishing world by storm he racked his brains for days searching for a graphic fictional surname for his megalomaniac villain. Eventually he found it rather close to home. 'Blofeld!' he cried at last, inspired by memories of Henry's formidable mother. Mrs Blofeld, it is said, enjoyed the private joke very much.

In America a superb writer called George Plimpton has made a career out of infiltrating the ranks of professional golf, baseball, football and boxing to record the emotions of the dumb performer suddenly embroiled in top-level sport. He has no counterpart in Britain. Playing golf against Gary Player in Johannesburg doesn't count since he was going out for a practice round anyway and my fluke birdie four at the 6th didn't exactly elevate one to the senior-wrangler ranks of the golf correspondents. Anyway I later played against Bridget Gleason and Jane Connachan, respectively the girl golf prodigies of Ireland and Scotland, at Killarney and Turnberry, and was steamrollered 6 and 4 on each occasion. Miss Gleason, then all of twelve, became so bored with the proceedings that she climbed a tree along the 12th fairway.

There was marginally greater, though short-lived, success in the only foot-race to which I have been sufficiently presumptious to challenge a professional footballer. Inevitably it took place abroad in the small hours of the morning when the last bar had closed and delusions of athletic grandeur are running rampant.

The city was Milan, the footballer Jimmy Greaves, and the period that in which the only way a British soccer star could make money appropriate to his talent was to emigrate. Greaves emigrated from Chelsea to Italy, hated every day of what he had let himself in for and was only happy in the evenings when he could let his hair down with a small team of British sportwriters who were also down there to report his daily battles with Nereo Rocco, Milan's dogmatic team manager.

The night of the Great Race had been less one of nostalgia for Old London Town than an incandescent investigation into such new diversions as Milan had to offer. Apart from La Scala they were thin on the ground.

The race was therefore home-made entertainment, along a dimly-lit arcade flanking a row of fashionable shops. It was probably 130 yards long and though Greaves was just leading at the 100 either some sixth sense or uncanny eyesight caused him to slacken his pace. Your correspondent, triumphant at a professional footballer's failure to sustain the course, whooped past and ran full pelt into an unseen spiked chain that blocked off the exit. It struck him fractionally below the progenitive region and caused him to describe a complete somersault before rendering himself unconscious on the hard road that leads out towards Florence.

Jimmy Greaves was extremely solicitous about summoning taxis, helping a British reporter to bed and summoning night porters bearing recuperative measures of brandy. He was transferred back to Tottenham Hotspur shortly afterwards, moved on to West Ham and later became a helpless alcoholic. His recovery is one of the joys of my life for he is a true friend and one of the few footballers of modern times to illuminate a field with sheer instinctive genius.

Participation in other sports, apart from trying to avoid bulls in a street called the Estefeta in Pamplona, Spain, in the second week of July every year, has been of a more submissive nature. In other words you sit or lie there helplessly wondering how you have got yourself into another fine mess and asking is it really worth all this to generate some thirty paragraphs in a newspaper?

One of these occasions was in Surin, an overnight train ride up from Bangkok, where the annual sports carnival features elephants racing against one another and engaging two hundred of the king's strongest soldiers in a lopsided tug-of-war which the elephant usually wins. In the interval they call for volunteers to lie in the dust in the centre of the enormous arena and permit the elephants to step over them in a ceremonial plod-past.

Actually there is nothing to it other than the nagging awareness that if one of the string of half a dozen elephants puts a foot on instead of over you, you will be squashed like a fly hit by a copy of *Tatler*.

When it is over you have developed a life-long love affair with elephants. They are the gentlest of God's awkward-shaped creatures. You feel a faint wetness as the trunk comes over first and then the leading foot actually brushes your chest. The elephant's perception through his sole is so sensitive that it is like being flicked by a feather duster. They have infinitely sad eyes but they never make a mistake, which is probably why so many of them live to such a venerable age.

Quite another sensation, which also has little connection with conventional sport, is to fly with the RAF's stupendous aerobatic team, the Red Arrows.

By the time you drive up to the guardhouse of their headquarters at Kemble in Gloucestershire you are in such a state of nerves that nothing would please you more than to be detained as a Soviet spy.

'Oh, yes,' says a gentleman with knife-edge creases all over him, 'they are expecting you, sir.'

There is much worse to come. After pushing a few baked beans around a plate during the least-wanted lunch in your life, you are escorted to a room containing what appears to be an electric chair and a matter-of-fact executioner to go with it.

'Now, sir,' the executioner says, holding all four aces, 'are you completely acquainted with the function of an ejector seat?'

You admit meekly that owing to a lifetime in trains, buses, tube-trains, cars, even rather fast sports cars, you have never previously encountered an ejector seat.

Completely in charge now, the instructor recites: 'In the event of an emergency, sir, you will, on receipt of the order "Get out", pull these wire butterfly-wings above your head which release the canopy. You will then pull hard on this metal ring between your legs which will fire you out of the plane. The next thing you know is that you will be floating down to earth under a parachute, probably in the vicinity of Cirencester. By the way, sir, one piece of advice. Try and keep your legs together as you go out or else I'm afraid we may find them left behind in the wreckage.'

Swallowing hard to keep half a dozen baked beans in position you are about to leave the room when the ejector-seat instructor throws in a deadly postscript.

'By the way, sir, if you receive the instruction "Get out f****** quick", don't worry about the butterfly wings over your head. There won't be a lot of time. Just pull the ring between your legs. It will blast you straight through the canopy, no problem, but you might have a slight headache afterwards.'

Thus reassured you haul yourself into one of those beautiful planes, taxi down to the end of the runway and take off, marvelling that these brilliant pilots can fly wing-tip to wing-tip, nose to tail, under the stress of G-forces that convince the layman that a five-ton weight is being remorselessly lowered on to his head.

I have enjoyed the privilege of flying four times with the Red Arrows, in the care of Squadron Leaders Mike Phillips and Mike Whitehouse, and have thus had the rare opportunity of looking upwards and seeing the roof of Ely Cathedral overhead. It is the second-best sensation I have yet experienced.

It remains an academic point whether sportswriters are morally justified in making critical judgments about sportsmen but, in the case of the Red Arrows anyway, the words would only appear in *The Celestial Times*.

3
BAY
3

Chapter Three

STUMBLING AMONG THE GREAT

In the nervous early days it can be awesome to realize that last week's idol has become today's source of information and possibly next year's good friend. You learn, too, that the bigger they are the more generous they are likely to be. Muhammad Ali, Pele, Jack Nicklaus, Richie Benaud, Henry Cooper and James Hunt were much kinder to young reporters than many of the squeaky tennis players who will never see the last 16 at Wimbledon.

It is the same in the Press box. There was once a gentleman on *The Times* who used to stare at newcomers from a distance and then ask someone else which school the young man had been educated at. If it happened to be one of a number of establishments famed for racquets and

OUT WHICH SCHOOL
ONE WENT TO. THERE'S
DEAR.

rampaging homosexuality he would engage the newcomer in conversation. If it were not he would never speak to him. The old fool, alas, is dead now. He was an unending source of amusement and, happily, in the vast minority.

Meeting idols is always a risk. You can't help looking for feet of clay, stinginess at the bar or dandruff. Meeting Keith Ross Miller, just *meeting* him that is, was the biggest moment yet. His opening words were: 'What are you having?' He appeared to be buying drinks for the entire bar, two-thirds of the cricket-watching crowd outside and paying for them with a crumpled bunch of fivers and tenners which he pulled out of a hip pocket as though they were redundant bus tickets.

By then Keith Miller was writing cricket, between horse-race meetings, for the *Daily Express*, but as idols went, none had come greater. Neville Cardus, in a memorable profile, had called him the 'Australian In Excelsis' and that was just about it. There was his wartime career as a night-fighter pilot which made him slightly larger than death, let alone life. There was the thrilling fast bowling and electrifying batting. But above all there was the style.

Merely watching Miller come down the steps to bat was a lesson in how to make the enemy feel two-feet tall. Reputedly having usually changed straight from dinner jacket and black tie into cricket flannels, bat jammed almost vertically under his left arm as he dragged on his gloves with his teeth, he would suddenly toss back his hair, glance at the sky as though checking on whether the day were worthy of his attention and then smile. A generation of schoolboy cricketers tried to imitate it but unfortunately few of them were six-foot-one, bronzed and totally unconcerned at the prospect of the flak that was about to fly at them.

At our first meeting, which by coincidence was on the Southampton ground where I had failed to lay a bat on Tom Dean, I asked Miller whether he recalled hitting three successive balls out of the ground for six, a feat I had wisely played truant from school to witness. 'No,' said Keith, and added, using the great Australian adjective with perfect politeness, 'all these bloody grounds look the same to me.'

Bobby Simpson, subsequently an Australian Test captain, recalls the ultimate in Miller's total lack of interest in boring detail. Recruited from Western Australia to New South Wales to accelerate a career as his country's newest prodigy, Simpson found himself playing his first match before a huge crowd in Sydney Cricket Ground under Miller's unlikely captaincy. The regular captain was injured and Miller, surprisingly, had been named as deputy.

'Walking down the steps to go out to field,' Simpson remembers, 'a curious thing happened. The gateman suddenly stopped Keith and said: "Mr Miller, do you happen to know that you are taking twelve men out there?"

'What had happened, of course, was that Keith had completely forgotten to nominate a twelfth man. It was a hell of a problem to solve in a split second. Who was he going to drop? A fast bowler, a spinner, *me*? Keith never batted an eyelid. He simply turned round and said: "Look, would one of you chaps kindly piss off." '

Bobby Simpson survived. He followed Miller into the centre of that vast, lovely ground and waited for the great man, who was going to open the bowling himself, to set his field. Would it be three slips and two gullies or two leg slips, two slips and one gully? Would he, even at this stage, put in a precautionary fine-leg?

Keith Miller's tactical strategy was revealed as he walked back to deliver the first ball of the match. He turned his head over his shoulder and shouted: 'Scatter.'

Miller's English contemporary and counterpart was Denis Compton, another idol with eccentric habits like scoring 300 runs in 181 minutes and drinking a large brandy at half-time in a Cup Final. They were more than colourful heroes to fire a youthful imagination. They were men who played ferociously hard but with a generosity of spirit and respect for the rules that could provide a useful yardstick when writing years later about John McEnroe at Wimbledon.

Some heroes, inevitably, turned out to be rather more curious, including the slickly brilliantined man who played such cultured, economic football at full-back for Southampton in the days when the admission price for schoolboys was, I think, a shilling. Alf Ramsey was to leave our neck of the woods for higher things with Tottenham Hotspur and England but his genius, of course, was for tactical management. He transformed a spare-parts team called Ipswich into Football League champions and took England to World Cup victory in 1966, and you don't do that by guesswork or luck.

Nor, certainly, do you do it by courting the Press. Sir Alfred Ramsey, as he quite rightly now is, didn't enjoy the company of a lot of people. These included most Scotsmen, all foreigners and many sportswriters. He had his favourites among the reporters but I was not one of them. I have never learned exactly what I did to plunge so deeply into his black books but I surmise it was an interview I had with one of his former Southampton colleagues and included in an hour-long TV profile-documentary about my old hero.

'H'Alf', recalled his ex-team mate proudly, 'was always gonny get on, wonny? Blimey, he used to talk like wot I do now, dinny? But H'Alf was a cut above the rest of us. He wennorf and took helecution lessons, see, and look where 'e is nah.'

Where Sir Alfred was shortly after that was looking thunderously at a documentary that eulogized his achievements. He was as conscious of his clipped, precise accent as he was acutely sensitive about his working-class origins which, to my mind, made his success and his knighthood all the more creditable.

I preferred the down-to-earth Alf who was approached by a microphone-waving radio reporter in jazzy shirt and co-respondent shoes as soon as the defending England World Cup team of 1970 touched down in Mexico City.

'Hello, Sir Ramsey,' greeted the bouncing, grinning radio man. 'I am now going to interview you for the nation.'

'Ho no,' replied Sir Ramsey, 'you bleedin' aint.'

Another member of the British upper classes who made an indelible impression on the sportswriters fortunate enough to travel with him on the only freebooting adventure of his distinguished life was Bernard Marmaduke Fitzalan-Howard, 16th Duke of Norfolk, Earl Marshal of England and, amazingly, manager of the England cricket team that toured Australia in the dreadful British winter of 1962–63.

The Duke just happened to be sitting in the committee room at Lord's one summer's day when they were discussing who should captain the England side on the forthcoming tour. Ted Dexter was favourite but the Dexter of those days had the reputation of being a haughty, difficult young man who would instantly alienate the Australian Press.

'Anyone can manage the team,' someone observed, 'but who can manage Dexter?'

'I can,' muttered the Duke. It was to prove one of the more significant throwaway lines of modern cricket. When you are Earl Marshal of England, responsible to the monarch for the nation's ceremonial and protocol, it is not all that simple to slip abroad on a five-month cricket expedition. Telephone calls were made from Lord's to Buckingham Palace and the Duchess of Norfolk who, naturally, was living in Sussex. An hour later Bernard Marmaduke had been appointed boss.

We flew with the team to Aden and there boarded the liner *Canberra* to proceed to Fremantle, Western Australia.

On only the second night at sea the Duke of Norfolk revealed his willingness to establish good relations with the Press by throwing a private dinner party for the English cricket correspondents covering the tour. He was a warm, generous man with an expressionless low-key wit and absolutely no conception of what the lower classes had to put up with in homes of fewer than 200 rooms.

As soon as we sat down he insisted on putting us at ease. 'Look,' he said, 'I want this to be a completely informal tour. When you address me you will merely call me "Sir".'

His Grace had hardly been a schoolboy hero of mine for I knew little about him other than his genius for staging pageantries like the Coronation which made an envious world admit there was no nation who could do it like the British. By the end of the Australian tour he was certainly a hero. He had much time for the sheepshearers of the outback, far less for Melbourne's pushy social hostesses, mostly chose Freddie Trueman as his golfing partner and

never allowed the sun's relative position to the yardarm to dictate his drinking habits. I believe he enjoyed himself hugely except during one painful and disgraceful episode.

Shortly before Christmas the Duke flew back to Britain for a brief visit. The Australian Press lambasted him for exercising a privilege not available to other members of the touring party. They accused him of desertion and hammered him again on his return. He was deeply wounded but said nothing by way of mitigation.

He was in no position to explain the facts. These were that by command of the Queen he had returned to London to organize and rehearse the street ceremonial for the funeral of the ailing Winston Churchill at some ungodly hour of a winter's morning.

Late one evening, back in Australia, he entrusted the truth of it to a few of us on the strict understanding that we did not reveal it while he was still alive. Churchill's funeral was his last mega-production. The grand old duke is also dead now, and that's another hero gone.

Chapter Four

JAPS AND OTHER EX-COMMUNICATIONS

The long and occasionally hilarious history of what Americans call communication malfunctions was richly endowed by the mildly reproving telegram Mark Twain once fired off to the editor of the Associated Press. He had, after all, just opened a newspaper and read his own obituary notice. Twain, who happened to be in sturdy health at the time, cabled: 'Your report of my death was grossly exaggerated.'

I know precisely how the author of the obituary felt having also killed off a man long before his time. The circumstances were a million light years from being amusing.

As the southbound train pulled into Stafford station late on a February afternoon in 1958 the newspaper sellers were racing along the platform in an unusual state of excitement. You had to turn the local evening paper sideways for the explanation. There, in a few lines in the stop-press, was the news that the aircraft carrying Manchester United home from a European Cup-tie had crashed on the runway in Munich. They were then the most famous club side in the world. Many of their players were personal friends, as were all the sportswriters who followed them everywhere. Among them was Frank Taylor, the man who had done more than anyone to get me my first job on a national newspaper, the *News Chronicle*. He was the complete newspaperman who relaxed as hard as he worked.

No train had been so dilatory in its progress from Stafford to London. No taxi had ever hit so many red traffic lights on the way down to Fleet Street. There is no building in the world so thrilling as a newspaper office when an immense story is breaking tight to an edition time. It is so often news of tragedy or disaster that there is no time, amid the controlled chaos, for the remotest sentiment. Until, that is, you are tersely told that Frank Taylor has been killed and you have thirty-five minutes to write his obituary.

It was not the easiest story I have ever written but it caught the first edition as a side-bar tribute alongside the huge headlines that were to become the epitaph to a football team of glittering class. It was already too late to recall those early editions when, on one of the many phone-lines open to Munich, we received a curious message. 'Look,' said one of the reporters on the spot, 'there's a badly-injured guy in hospital by the name of Alexander who shouldn't have been on the plane at all. There's no record of him on the passenger list. Who the hell can he be?'

Who the hell he was was our colleague Frank Taylor.

In the fire that engulfed the plane's wreckage Frank's passport had been badly burned. The 'Alexander' the German police had managed to decipher from the charred remnants was the Christian name of Frank's younger son, which had been included on his father's passport for a family holiday abroad.

Frank Taylor recovered to survive the now-dead *News Chronicle*. He became president of the world sportswriters' organization, still graces the sports pages of the *Daily Mirror* and from time to time glances at the now-yellowing newspaper cutting that somewhat exaggerated his death. From time to time we have a quiet drink in some bar around the world to celebrate a quarter of a century of extra-time.

In British newspapers communication malfunctions are known by another name altogether. They are rarely understood by top executives who return from lunch at the Savoy Grill to a warm office to discover there's still no word from the reporter they sent to the North Pole yesterday with £500 in travellers' cheques and a kiss on the cheek. Most home-based executives are convinced that all trees in Borneo and most rock-faces in the Alaska Range are fitted with telephones which you pick up, talk to a honey-tongued international operator who speaks English as though she's been to Cheltenham Ladies' College and are instantly connected with base. This is not necessarily an accurate assumption.

It was certainly not true when some 800 sportswriters descended on Zaire, formerly the Belgian Congo, to cover one of the greatest fights of modern times in probably the most bizarre setting since the David-Goliath mis-match. Seeking international publicity, President Mobutu decided to invest such public funds as he hadn't already siphoned into his private Swiss bank accounts in a world heavyweight title match between Muhammad Ali and the gargantuan George Foreman. If I appear less than charitable to Zaire's president it is only because one of his minions had me arrested for writing about the bribery and corruption that are the genuine national sports of his disgusting one-party jungle.

For a promoter bent on getting his name into newspapers around the world, President Mobutu's grasp of the electronic communications systems necessary to bring this about were on a par with the average witchdoctor's.

The two fighters were quartered in villas at N'Sele, forty miles from the capital, Kinshasa. Our spirits soared when we were ushered into a spacious modern building which had been converted into a Press centre. They rose still higher when we saw two banks of gleaming new telex machines on which we could tap out our daily dispatches directly back to our offices during the ten days of build-up to the fight. They fell abruptly when we discovered there were no wall points into which they could be plugged. Twelve telex machines without electricity have the equivalent value of a heliograph in thick fog.

There was worse to come at the ringside. Reporting big fights, round by round as they happen, is one of the most demanding exercises in sportswriting. Usually, back home, your newspaper is already printing as you feed in your story, paragraph by paragraph, for later editions. There is hardly a moment to scrawl a note, none at all to construct the kind of sentence you would hope to produce with time and a typewriter. You crouch there, attempting to shield the mouthpiece of your telephone from the noisy pandemonium around you, praying that the gentleman back in London who takes your words on a typewriter can actually hear them. At the really big fights you can rarely hear him. It is like yelling into a force-ten gale on a very dark night.

From Zaire it was precisely that. Its telephone system was slightly better than its telex. It at least stood the strain for the opening three rounds. Unfortunately it was the eighth round before Muhammad Ali at last came off the ropes to hit Foreman with the historic punch that sent him sprawling, ended his career and confounded hundreds of confident predictions. What I did not know at the time was that for the last five rounds I had been dictating into a telephone as dead as a stuffed carp.

Thankfully the *Daily Mail* had organized a back-up operation. My colleague Peter Moss was in the Post Office Tower in London watching the live pictures come in from the Congo for relay to BBC Television. He grabbed a telephone and completed our report.

At least we were luckier than the Fleet Street rival who at the Munich Olympic Games in 1972 bravely entrusted his entire day's dispatch to the normally infallible German telex system. It probably read very well to the Bond Street florists who watched in astonishment as it stuttered out of their machine.

The telex replaced the cable, a more expensive but at the same time more graceful means of communication for the correspondent who wasn't actually writing under fire. It was virtually an elongated telegram and in less democratic days you were encouraged to phone the cable office in most large overseas cities and request that a uniformed messenger be sent to your hotel room to collect your words. This was particularly popular among vintage English cricket correspondents who liked to compose their 'pieces' – cricket correspondents never write 'reports' and detest being described as sportswriters – while wearing Paisley-patterned silk dressing-gowns and sipping gin-and-tonic. Many of them would have preferred to have been Lord Curzon.

A giant among them, of course, was Sir Neville Cardus whose insistence on never allowing a fact to impair an elegant essay made him one of the most elegant essayists ever to write about sport in the English language. His meticulousness was such that in cabling his pieces from Australia he insisted, regardless of the horrendous additional expense to the always impoverished *Guardian*, on spelling out each punctuation mark in words like this: 'Hutton comma batting capless in the bewildering heat comma struck Lindwall past coverpoint semi colon Compton comma the colour of tawny port comma restrained his buccaneering instinct stop paragraph.'

Since cables were costed by the word, the *Guardian* management on one unwise occasion decided to send Sir Neville a gentle message suggesting a practical economy. 'You send words,' it read, 'we insert punctuation.' It elicited one of the better ripostes of our time. 'I send punctuation,' cabled back the outraged Cardus, 'you insert words.' He continued sending both.

The saga of communication foul-ups by telephone deserves a four-volume study. Copy-takers, who sit there with headphones and typewriter awaiting words yelled,

...AND A BEAUTIFUL
LEFT HOOK FROM
ALI......

gabbled or sometimes slurred at them from telephone kiosks or Press boxes all over the world, are mostly men who read Machiavelli in the original Italian and unravel *The Times* crossword in twenty minutes. They generally have a low opinion of sportswriters, regarding us as on the same intellectual plane as garbage collectors. It would be libellous to suggest that they occasionally help to compound our own errors by the deliberate slip of a typing finger, but strange things have happened. None is stranger than that which baffled many readers of a *Wolverhampton Express and Star* Saturday football edition.

Covering a disappointing home performance by Wolverhampton Wanderers, the paper's footbali writer, dictating back to base as the game was in progress, found himself delivering the phrase: 'Chinks began to appear in the Wolves defence.'

'No, cross that out,' he hurriedly told the copy-taker. It was a commendable erasure since the Wolverhampton Wanderers' manager at the time was Sammy Chung, who despite a long career in English soccer was still by surname and appearance unmistakeably of Chinese origin.

Not wishing to cause offence or fall foul of the Race Relations Board, the reporter amended the phrase to read: 'Gaps began to appear in the defence.'

What finally appeared in print to explain Wolves' home defeat gave the disconcerting impression that an invasion of Japs had suddenly swarmed all across the penalty area.

Copy-takers can be scathingly critical of sportswriters' syntax, ad-libbing thoughts into hopefully coherent sentences in the high-pressure closing moments of night football matches. It is a craft that requires cool nerves and no interruptions and the two outstanding masters of it in Fleet Street in recent years have been Geoffrey Green, of *The Times*, and Jeffrey Powell, of the *Daily Mail*.

Powell had his fiercest engagement with a copy-taker the evening he was dictating from the Liverpool Press gallery in the dying minutes of a tumultuous European Cup-tie. 'Liverpool,' he was saying, 'strode deeper into Europe at Anfield last night. . . ' when a sudden scream down the telephone halted him.

'Stop,' yelled the copy-taker, a much-loved Pakistani who typed rather faster than he acquainted himself with the names of English football grounds. 'You cannot possibly say that.'

'Listen,' Powell yelled back, 'you just keep typing and we'll argue later.'

'No,' retorted the Pakistani, 'I cannot put down things which are totally ungrammatical.'

'What the hell,' demanded a now-apoplectic Powell, 'are you raving on about?'

'Mr Powell,' explained the Karachi-born copy-taker with exaggerated patience, 'the word "field" begins with a consonant and not a vowel. It is therefore quite incorrect to say that Liverpool played at an field. It must be that Liverpool played at a field.'

'Certainly,' said Powell. 'You just put "a field" and then start typing. Fast.'

Writing about sport is a lovely way to spend a lifetime. It's the communications that cause thrombosis. Shortly before Christmas 1979 I was sent to Yaounde, the capital of Cameroon, West Africa, to eavesdrop on a series of meetings between the Supreme Council for Sport in Africa and a visiting Soviet delegation. The Russians were discussing just how much bribe money the African nations wanted not to boycott, and thus wreck, the 1980 Olympic Games in Moscow.

Getting to Yaounde was comparatively simple. Getting home in time for Christmas was another matter. Air tickets with confirmed flight places, even when accompanied by high-denomination notes for the subsequent personal use of the counter-clerk, were greeted with high-pitched laughter and the advice to come back either next week or the week after.

A good friend helped out. We flew as far as Douala and booked into a hotel intent on battering our way to London, Amsterdam, Munich, Vienna, anywhere, the following morning. I booked a telephone call to my wife in London to appraise her of the problem.

At 3am the phone rang. 'Your call to London,' announced the night clerk. There followed a symphony of high-pitched whistles, atmospherics and a snatch of conversation between two ladies speaking in French. I fell asleep with the phone off the hook.

At 3.05am in Knightsbridge, London, the phone rang. 'Hold on for a call from West Africa,' announced the operator. There followed a symphony of high-pitched whistles, atmospherics and snatches of conversation between two ladies speaking in French. Sarah listened for a while and then fell asleep with the phone off the hook.

At 5am some ghost shook me by the shoulder. The telephone was still in my hand. I realized we had probably just made the world's first two-hour £140 phone call in which neither party had spoken a single word.

ZZZZZZ
ZZZZZZZ

"HE PROBABLY CAN'T SLEEP WITHOUT THAT FAMILIAR SOUND BESIDE HIM."

Chapter Five

THE CASE FOR ABSTINENCE

I used to believe that journalists could drink until I fell among jazz musicians and discovered we are hardly third division. Nonetheless bars remain the reporter's Mission Control. He is hired in them, fired in them, and uses them rather as Karl Marx used the Reading Room at the British Museum: to elicit information that hopefully will later shake the world.

One of my early introductions to a Fleet Street bar starred a show-business columnist of Irish extraction and a legendary capacity who returned to his office full of five hours of liquid inspiration and addressed his typewriter with the same vigorous panache that Miss Eileen Joyce used to apply to the crashing initial chords of the Grieg A minor piano concerto. Unfortunately, his aim was considerably less deft and hc jammed his fingers in the keyboard so irretrievably that City of London fire officers had to be summoned to cut him free. 'Don't worry,' someone said, 'it happens all the time.' In fact it happens far less frequently than it used to, which is not to allege that Fleet

Street has entirely sobered up.

One of the more historic and significant sportswriting binges deserves slightly more attention than its consequences were later to receive. It started around five o'clock on the afternoon of Sunday 23 June 1968, in a flat just north of Fleet Street, and was roaring along quite sociably at 2.30 the following morning when I made the unpopular unilateral decision to take a taxi home. In retrospect this was an amazingly responsible act since at 11.30 the same morning England and Australia were to resume hostilities on the fourth day of the Lord's Test Match.

It was the sort of day you needed such wits as you have about you. It was the 200th Test between the oldest enemies in cricket and Australia were promptly bowled out for 78, their lowest score in England since 1912. Even *The Times* promoted the sensation to its front page, with photographs of the fall of all ten wickets. What neither *The Times* nor any other newspaper spelled out was that a contributory factor to the batting débâcle may just have been the presence of almost every member of the Australian team at the Sunday night to Monday morning party, celebrating the wedding of one of Australia's most notoriously hard-living cricket writers. Many were still there at the time of my departure and revealing marked reluctance to go anywhere before the last bottle of champagne had had its neck wrung. One of them confided subsequently that he found it disturbingly difficult even to see where the stumps were when he walked out to bat.

In the circumstances, 78 was possibly an heroic total but equally heroic, I like to think, were the efforts of the sportswriters of both countries in attributing Australia's totally unexpected collapse to a freak combination of low cloud-base and sudden rush of warm southerly air which produced the rare atmospheric conditions in which a cricket ball swings like a boomerang. This seemed to satisfy an English public who were ecstatic anyway and go some way to appeasing those Australians who rated it their blackest national day since Gallipoli. It is not often that the sporting Press so protects international sporting idols but on this occasion there was the self-interest that comes from complicity. Beyond that, Australian cricketers down the years have proved themselves friendlier and less sensitive to honest criticism than most sportspersons.

That Monday evening at Lord's a hastily prepared scroll was presented by English sportswriters to the Australian bridegroom who had given the party, acknowledging his services to English cricket. It was not quite the end of the affair.

Some years later, on the retirement of the Australian batsman who had had difficulty focussing on the stumps when he walked out at Lord's, I wrote some of the above facts in the *Daily Mail*. It caused a mild sensation in Australia where it was instantly reprinted in several newspapers. Reporters immediately contacted the Australian cricket administrator who had been team manager on the 1968 tour to England. Having failed at the time even to wink his thanks that our silence had saved him the unpleasant experience of sending several of his players home, he ascribed the story to the lurid imagination of a typical Pommie pressman. Well, here I am, a typical Pommie pressman who was *at* the party.

Trials by alcohol, however, are not always the prerogative of the reporter. If jazzmen drink more than journalists, there are Soviet Union party officials who can drink both professions under the table. The 1980 Olympic Games in Moscow were, by their propagandist nature, a comparatively sober celebration of all that is good in Soviet life outside Communism, anti-Semitism, a secret police system and forced labour camps. This was hardly the case six years earlier when as part of their campaign to bring the Games to Moscow they invited a delegation of twenty-three sportswriters from all over the Western world to tour the Soviet Union for a fortnight and write eulogies about the Russian sports system which would influence the votes of the International Olympic Committee.

It was my first visit to Russia and the initial hint of the arduous trencherman challenge that lay ahead was not even delayed till we got there. I made bold enough, over East German airspace, to ask the thirteen-stone Aeroflot air hostess who bore a remarkable resemblance to Rocky Marciano, for a post-lunch brandy. She returned not with the miniature measure served by British Airways, TWA and other parsimonious airlines, but a full off-licence-sized bottle of Hine.

This, as it proved, was mere net-practice for the lunches, receptions, dinners and full-scale banquets that comprised most of our itinerary from Moscow, via Kiev to Tblisi, in Georgia. There were frequently five different-sized glasses to the right of each table-place, the first of which was constantly being refilled with vodka for official one-gulp toasts to everyone from the latest Soviet cosmonaut to the Nuremburg hangman. The whole objective of Russian hostmanship is to immobilize guests in the shortest possible time and thus strike a blow for peasant hardheadedness. To be fair to our team the only conspicuous Soviet victory was achieved at a moonlit open-air dinner under pine trees on the banks of the Dnieper when the sports editor of America's *Atlanta Constitutional* crashed headlong over the silver and Imperial dining service before even the first course had been served.

Our champion was a small Dublin sportswriter named Seamus Martin whose composure after all the Soviet Union could funnel into him was such that 18-stone Georgian alcoholics gazed at him with the awe that most of us would gaze upon, say, the Rose Window in Notre Dame. His fulminations against the Soviet system in public places late each evening were such that the KGB man responsible for our welfare was a nervous wreck long before the end of the tour. It didn't matter much, KGB men are ten a rouble and Moscow won the Olympic Games anyway.

Drinking and writing, of course, has about as much future as drinking and driving. You may feel like Dostoyevsky or even James Hunt at the time but 11pm's brilliant epigrams invariably read like bad commercial radio jingles over breakfast.

Several of the most literate men in British writing, let alone sportswriting, are or were the first men to reach the bar at close of play. Hugh McIlvanney, of *The Observer*, has been known to outsit all opposition, but what the propagators of the romantic Fleet Street myths never see are the Perrier water days behind 'Don't disturb' signs on hotel doors from Sydney to Acapulco. Within, a Calvinistic conscience is at work, putting into thirty-seven words

emotions that lesser writers cannot capture in a column. It is about perceptive imagery and the intrinsic value of the verb over the adjective. It is hard, grinding work even if you have time on your side but happily the labour is rarely witnessed.

John Arlott, now retired, and Henry Longhurst, now dead, were big drinkers and also mentors to two generations of British sportswriters.

'They tell me,' drawled John Arlott one evening in a Cambridge hotel, 'that I only have to keep sober to win this one.' He drank two glasses of sherry which hardly touched the sides and we drove down to the Cambridge Union. It was at the height of famous D'Oliveira Affair which brought the meaning of South Africa's apartheid policy home to those still innocent enough to believe that sport could remain isolated from politics. The Union building was packed and Arlott, speaking last, put his left hand in the pocket of what appeared to be a pre-war shooting jacket and spoke without hesitation or note.

The conviction matched the faultless English. Overwhelmingly he won the night and returned to the hotel to make up for lost pre-dinner drinks.

Henry Longhurst, the most literate commentator to describe any sport on any English-language television network, was more than once seen pressing small dark patterns on the wallpaper of hotel lounges late at night under the optimistic impression that he was summoning the lift. He never recollected such minor aberrations in the morning and was never embarrassed when people told him. 'Dear boy,' he'd say, 'we are all as the good Lord made us. On the other hand always remember to jot down the odd word or two or things that people tell you, however drunk you are, so that you can recall it in the morning. That's our stock-in-trade.' I have heard earnest men attempt to elevate journalism to some kind of sacred vocation but, as usual, Longhurst had it right. It is simply the game of story-telling and he was its master.

In a ubiquitous career from top-class amateur golf to the House of Commons, Henry Longhurst had many finest hours. I was privileged to see one of them on the eve of a Ryder Cup golf match between the United States and Britain at the El Dorado Country Club in California.

The official dinner was attended by more than 500 of what then were known as the Beautiful People. The lavishly embossed menu, listing the after-dinner speakers, bore the Stars and Stripes, the Union Jack and an alarming item of information. The second speaker was Bob Hope, the third Henry Longhurst.

Following Bob Hope in the oratory business is like walking on to the concert platform in the wake of Rubenstein. Hope made it no easier by being at the height of his form, firing out laconic one-liners honed by his battery of scriptwriters with the usual incomparable timing. It lasted ten minutes, brought the house down and was enough to make any speaker who had to follow *that* feign a heart attack.

When Henry Longhurst rose to his full five-foot-seven to reply on behalf of Great Britain he attracted nothing more than curiosity. It was long before he had become a cult figure on American television, his name and reputation were largely unknown and with his heavy jowels and Sussex landowner's complexion he looked rather like a bulldog which had struggled into his master's black tie and dinner jacket.

He cleared his throat, began: 'My Lords, ladies and gentlemen,' which is a rather uncommon form of address in California, and proceeded to hit them with a speech sheerly Churchillian in delivery, hilarious in content and so masterly in its command of language that even Bob Hope swivelled round in his chair to rivet his attention on this strange, squat Englishman. As Longhurst sat down his huge audience rose as one family to confer upon him the ultimate accolade of a minute-long standing ovation. It was a very proud moment if you happened to be British, even if we did proceed to make a horrible hash of the Ryder Cup.

It is quite possible that Henry had the customary couple of stiff ones to tune up for the ordeal. It is a matter of legend that two hours later, job done, he was relaxed to the degree that the construction of a sentence as complex as 'Good night' was definitely taxing his intellectual resources.

GOOD
NIGHT

BLUGGER
KIM II SHUNG...!
.... HIC!

I have only one happier drinking recollection and it comes from the strangest society on earth, which is Comrade President Kim Il Sung's North Korea from which all Western visitors, let alone capitalist jackal journalists, were rigidly banned during the thirty-four years from the end of World War II until 1979. The reason for this becomes apparent within a day of arrival. In three decades of absolute isolation the entire population has been brainwashed beyond even George Orwell's imagination. Every child is identically dressed in uniforms approved by Kim Il Sung, every adult refers to the gracious benefactions of Kim Il Sung in almost every sentence he speaks, world history has been rewritten by Kim Il Sung in such a way that Kim Il Sung emerges as its only sane leader, no restaurant, shop, office or hotel bedroom is without its beaming portrait of Kim Il Sung, a gilt statue of Kim Il Sung half as high as St Paul's dominates the capital, Pyongyang, you find a bound volume of Kim Il Sung's more significant utterances where you normally find a Gideon's Bible, Kim Il Sung's picture appears on the front page of every newspaper every day, no theatre production is about anything other than Kim Il Sung's military genius in keeping his peoples free and the first place they took us, naturally, was to the tarted-up hovel where Kim Il Sung was allegedly born. It bore a striking resemblance to a certain stable in Bethlehem and maybe that was the idea.

Obviously it didn't take long to get the general hang of who the top man around the place actually was, despite the fact that we were only there to report the 35th world table tennis championships.

Visiting sportswriters were paired off and placed in the care of a trusted interpreter and guide whose primary function was to make sure we never got within writing range of anything that suggested Kim Il Sung wasn't the greatest thing since one of his ancestors had personally engineered the birth of the cosmos.

My partner was Richard Eaton, of *The Times*, and our protector was Pak Ro Sung, a small, charming man who wore the obligatory Kim Il Sung fan club badge in his left lapel and greeted us each morning with the words: 'Our beloved leader Kim Il Sung wishes you another happy day in our fatherland.' Apart from his occasional denunciation of the imperalist warmonger Churchill, whom he insisted was American, Mr Pak was so genial that Eaton and I respectfully acknowledged his anxious requests to toe the line.

On May Day, however, the world table tennis championships were suspended so that we all could celebrate what Comrades Kim Il Sung, Marx and Engels, in strictly that order, had done for the working classes of the world. We were shunted off to Pyongyang's main park where sopranos, massed choirs, gymnasts and orators all dedicated their performances to you know who.

At midday Eaton and I invited Mr Pak to lunch. He declined. We insisted. It was, we pointed out, Kim Il Sung's big day and British courtesy demanded we entertained our only North Korean friend in the finest style our employers' money could buy. Mr Pak was visibly moved. He agreed and our black official car drove us down to a riverside restaurant where a miracle awaited. In addition to a bottle of North Korean vodka we searched for, found and bought a bottle of vermouth and two bottles of French burgundy that must have been there for years.

Mr Pak's protests that he only rarely touched alcohol naturally had to be brushed aside. We mixed powerful vodka-martinis at the table and made it clear we would doubt Mr Pak's patriotism if he did not drink with us as we celebrated the health of his leader, government, wife, mother, children and the Queen of England.

By four o'clock Mr Pak was wildly in favour of decadent Western habits. By 4.30 he pronounced himself incapably drunk. He staggered ahead of us to the car which was to take us to the State Circus where he suddenly fell sideways in his seat and snored like a horse throughout the most breathtaking trapeze acts in captivity.

At the interval we carried him quietly from the dress circle and instructed our driver to take him home. He was the nicest security policeman I have ever met.

Chapter Six

TRAVELS WITH MONTY

For a Cockney Jew with a lisp and only a tenuous grasp of either syntax or geography, Moses 'Monty' Fresco has come a very long way. To the bewilderment of those rivals who wear spotted neckerchiefs and desert boots and do dramatic things with lightmeters, he has won almost every international award available to the Press photographer. Monty usually snatches a quick look at the position of the sun and shoots.

His genius, apart from that, is for getting into homes and countries where Press photographers and reporters are definitely not welcome and then charming Mafia hit-men, retired Nazi warlords, mass murderers and paranoid dictators into posing for him. It is a magic talent that cannot be taught. A few years ago Prince Charles asked Monty to fly

up to Balmoral to snap the kilted portrait he wanted for his personal Christmas card. I wasn't present but it is a toss-up whether Monty addressed him as 'Your Worship' or 'Your Grace'.

He is an eccentric joy to work with and many Fleet Street foreign correspondents and sportswriters are swift to acknowledge they would still be hammering on unyielding doors if Monty's honours degrees in sheer cheek and cunning had not worked a miracle. I certainly am, and was never more so than in the curious episode of The Fight That Never Was.

A year after the Muhammad Ali-George Foreman world title fight in Zaire, ex-Sergeant Major but by then His Excellency Field Marshal Doctor Idi Amin Dada, VC, DSO, MC, president of neighbouring Uganda, determined that he, too, would go into the boxing promotion business. A brief agency message into the *Daily Mail* office announced that a month hence Britain's John Conteh would fight an unnamed American opponent in Kampala. Applications for official accreditation to witness this incredible event were invited. This was astonishing on two counts. Firstly a brief phone call to John Conteh in London immediately established that he had no intention of going. Secondly Uganda was closed, and had been, particularly to journalists, for months. The last *Daily Mail* writer to have visited Uganda had been Leslie Watkins who was escorted directly to jail without passing go and tediously roughed-up by Amin's heavies.

Amin just happened to be in the terminal stages of his dictatorial madness. Any colleague who didn't send effusive birthday messages was likely to be put to death by methods that made the Spanish Inquisition seem like euthanasia. Naturally, to newspaper bosses, this made him eminent interview material and who better to send down there than a sportswriter stumblebumming his way around under the pretence of looking for a boxing match? Who better to send with him, thank God, than Monty Fresco?

We arrived in Entebbe in a Hemingway sunrise. There were very few passengers on our plane and only two immigration officers who, while smartly uniformed, looked more intellectually equipped for goat-herding.

'Ang about,' commanded Monty. We hung about. Eventually Monty fumbled in his hand-baggage and produced a photograph of himself with President Amin. 'Follow me,' he said.

At the immigration barrier we were invited to leave. 'Old on a minute, dawling,' said Monty, shoving the photograph under the goat-herd's eyes, 'your guvnor's a

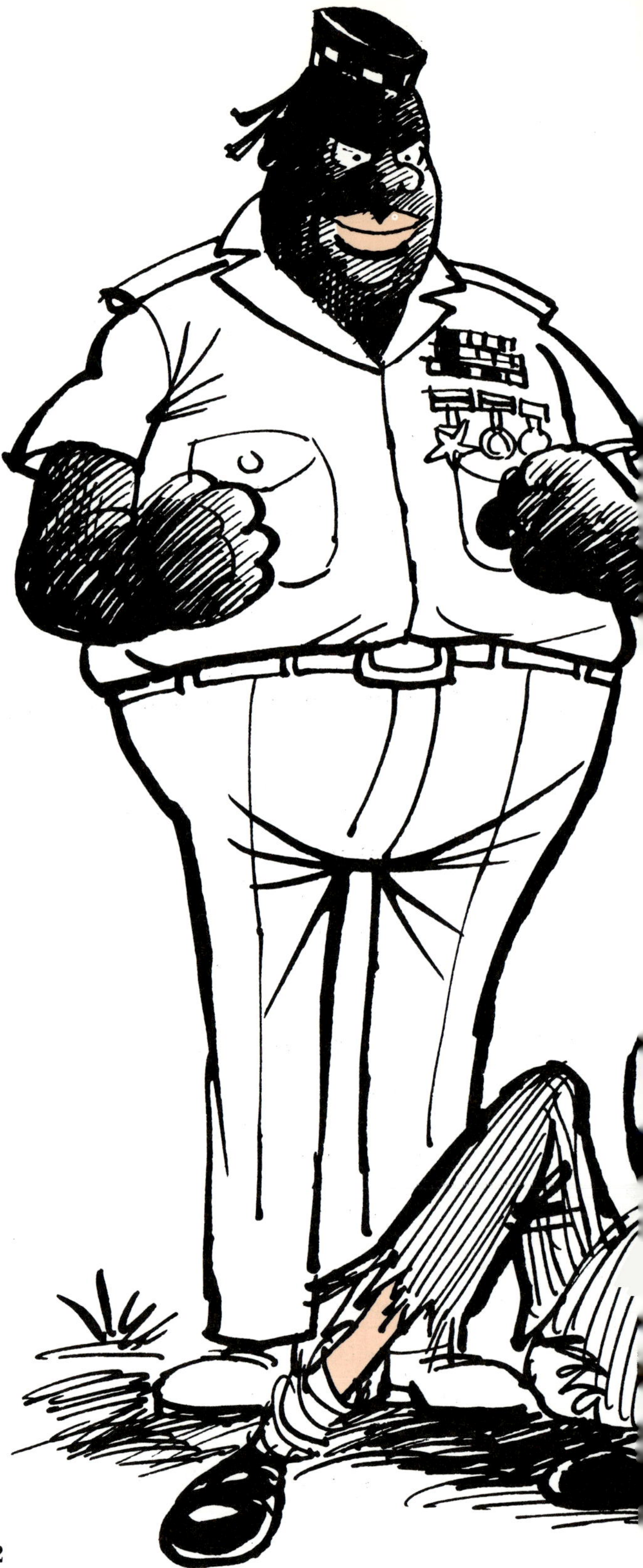

O.K. LET'S GET OUT OF HERE

personal mate of mine.' He started walking and thus we entered that desperate dictatorship. All we had to do now was find, interview and photograph the lunatic who ran it.

Each morning for five days we were required to report to a deeply suspicious Ministry of Information. Each morning for five days Monty dazzled them with his repertoire of circus tricks, monstrous lies, inquiries as to their grandmothers' health, tributes to their efficiency, solicitous advice about pension schemes and promises of permanent employment on the *Daily Mail* if only they would come up with Amin. On the sixth morning they did. We caught a private plane two hundred miles west to the village of Semliki and a little later a helicopter landed and the vast figure of Amin emerged, hand extended in gratitude that we had come to learn about his boxing match. His staff had been too petrified to inform him it was already cancelled.

Wearing one revolver, 36 bullets threaded through his belt, his paratrooper's wings and 12 other medal ribbons in addition to the self-awarded VC, DSO and MC, the then 48-year-old dictator compared his own boxing career favourably with Muhammad Ali's, pointing out that he was still heavyweight champion of both Uganda and East Africa since no challenger was prepared to fight him. He also confirmed that 30,000 Kampala hotel beds were awaiting overseas visitors to the Conteh fight, announced that he was about to build Africa's biggest stadium in order to stage the Commonwealth Games and gave me a message to deliver personally to the Queen at Buckingham Palace. 'I am very loyal to her,' explained the man who, at that stage, was alleged to have murdered only 25,000 of his brother Ugandans.

Monty was getting very fidgety about his picture. Amin was reluctant to strike a boxing pose until Fresco said: 'Lishen, my friend 'ere is a very fine boxah.' Amin stuck his hands up and for a few seconds we weaved and ducked around. 'That'll do,' Monty whispered suddenly, 'let's get out of 'ere.' We fled into Kenya on the next available plane.

Luck may have quite a deal to do with persistence. It can have even more to do with the photographer you are paired with. From the battlefields of Vietnam to the wings of the Miss World competition in London Monty Fresco has gone his own unique way. At the opening ceremony of the 1976 Olympic Games in Montreal, while his rivals were firing off in all directions, Fresco crouched motionless for more than an hour focussing a 600-millimetre Nikon on a single head in the British team standing 180 yards distant centre-field. Eventually the head turned, flashing a radiant smile illuminated still more by a beam of sunlight. Shot at 1/125th of a second at 5.6, Fresco's stunning picture of Princess Anne rightly earned him awards all over the world. It remains the greatest off-beat sports picture I have ever seen.

When Fresco is not taking pictures, explaining to his wife, Simmie, why he is just off abroad again for another unspecified period or beating down some Bangkok salesman to twenty per cent of the asking price for the oriental equivalent of three plaster wall ducks, he is playing poker, roulette or reading paperbacks whose laminex covers depict a sensual blonde with long legs, black stockings and a dagger sticking out of a diaphanous nightie.

But suddenly the cards are scattered, the book is flung aside and Fresco goes to work with an energy and resourcefulness that makes nonsense of his sixty years. Another occasion I had particular reason to be grateful for both came in Japan where we were sent at an hour's notice to cover the last dramatic act of James Hunt's duel with Niki Lauda for the 1976 Grand Prix drivers' championship. All went smoothly until the last mile of our journey when we drove into the village that lies at the foot of Mount Fuji, 120 miles outside Tokyo, and discovered that the hotel into which we had allegedly been booked for the hectic next four days did not even exist. There was not a bed within hours of the race circuit.

Monty contemplated the problem quietly, led the way to the nearest big hotel that did exist and confidently announced our arrival to an elderly male Japanese receptionist with astigmatism and fractured English. The old man took our passports, peered at our names, searched the register for anything that remotely resembled them and then shook his head. Monty's feigned perplexity deserved an Oscar.

He was still patiently explaining that he was closely related to Prince Philip, Duke of Edinburgh, when a fortuitous break arrived in the form of two German journalists from a Hamburg magazine. Their belligerence as they shouted their names panicked the old Japanese into near-blindness. Again he shook his head. A fearsome altercation broke out as one of the Germans yelled: 'It's impossible. These rooms have been booked for a week.'

And so they had. The receptionist, unfamiliar with the occidental alphabet, had missed them in the register. But Monty, hovering in the vicinity, had not. In the noisy confusion he produced a thick felt pen, obliterated the German names and substituted 'Fresco' and 'Wooldridge'.

As the Germans argued furiously with one another Monty carried the register to the now-cowering receptionist, produced our passports again and gently pointed out that the two calm Englishmen had, in fact, been booked in all the time. The old Jap brightened instantly, happy that he had at least two satisfied customers. He produced the room keys that for the next four days allowed us to live and work in oriental comfort. We never saw the Germans again. Fresco expressed no remorse. 'War repairs,' he said, mysteriously. 'Reparations, you mean?' I asked. 'No, just kicking Itler up the arse after all these years,' he said, closing the subject with intense satisfaction. Monty devoted a lot of time to World War II.

Language confusions have not always produced such happy results. At the 1972 Olympic Games in Munich I was stupid enough to believe I could still stagger along in the Russian I had learned as a guest of Her Majesty in my early twenties. Surprising as it may seem this was not in prison but a two-year term of National Service in a Royal Navy keen to train interpreters and translators for the coming conflict. Russian is not as difficult as it looks until you come to the verbs of motion, a grammatical Grand National course which sorts out real linguists from the apprentice.

Twenty years later a sudden rush of blood to the ego convinced me that I still remembered sufficient Russian to interview Olga Korbut in her native language not only for the *Daily Mail* but for BBC Television cameras. She was then still a tiny, capricious girl with huge eyes, a bobbing pigtail and the capacity to captivate the world with a style of gymnastics so original that some ten million schoolgirls around the globe immediately took up the sport. No single athlete since the war has had such inspirational effect.

The day before our interview I borrowed a Russian dictionary, swotted up the words I had either forgotten or never known and prepared my questions. Next morning, with the TV cameras set up on the small lawn in front of the Soviet team headquarters, I discovered to my enormous pride that this intriguing little elf could understand almost every word I said.

She responded like some Parisian coquette. The interview was a triumph in all but one respect. She responded so swiftly and colloquially to my ponderously-worded interrogation that I hardly understood a single phrase she uttered. As the distinguished television correspondent Clive James was to point out in no uncertain terms a few days later, it was an idiotic exercise.

However, we had established contact with the gorgeous Olga and eight years later, at the Moscow Olympics, there was to be an interesting sequel.

Early one evening, writing my daily Olympic column amid the cheap pine bugging devices of Moscow's biggest hotel, I received a phone call from an old friend inviting me to a party later that night. 'There will probably be someone there,' he said, 'you would like to meet again.'

It was a small apartment on the ninth floor of one of the barrack blocks that stand like battlements round the perimeter of Moscow. The flat was filled with loud Western pop music, open bottles of whisky, gin and vodka and a fascinating assembly of Russia's free-thinking middle-class. They included a leading brain surgeon, two principal dancers from the Bolshoi and, gyrating in a world of her own to the blaring music in the centre of the floor, Olga Korbut.

She had aged twenty years in eight. Married now with one small son, she had been summoned from Kiev without her family to appear as a former Heroine of Soviet Sport at the spectacular Olympic opening ceremony. But then she had been officially abandoned, a spent force so extraneous to the Soviet propaganda machine that she didn't even have tickets to attend the gymnastics competitions.

But the personality, if tinged with cynicism, remained intact. Yes, she recalled our ludicrous interview in Munich and even remembered that when the Soviet wardress-chaperone wasn't looking I had slipped her a bottle of scent. We had a drink together before she went back to dancing.

The telephone was in the bedroom next door. By prodigious luck Monty Fresco had just returned to his hotel room from a slogging day around the Olympic stadia. 'Gotcher, dawlin', he said, and half an hour later rang the apartment doorbell. He left his cameras amid a pile of coats, strolled into the living-room, immediately had the Bolshoi dancers in stitches and an hour later was dancing with Olga.

'Moy dyedooshka,' cried Olga and Monty, unaware of the Russian word for grandfather, said: 'Anythin' you say, dawlin', but what I'm going to do now is take some 'appy family snaps.' He disappeared into the hall, returned with his cameras and to the delight of everyone fired off roll after roll of film including a dozen shots of Olga dancing like the forgotten woman she was on the centre of the floor.

Eighteen hours later the scene was being printed across the two-page centre-fold spread in two million copies of the *Daily Mail*.

There was no deception about it. Next morning Olga Korbut came to our hotel and posed for Monty sitting demurely on the banks of the Moskva River. If he had asked her to attempt to scale the Kremlin Wall she would probably have done it. No other photographer got within a mile of her.

'Jesus,' said Monty, 'that's some woman.' That's true. What is also true is that Monty Fresco is some photographer.

Chapter Seven

FAME STARTS AT THE BUS STOP

There was a Saturday evening in 1972 when those checking their football pools during the results sequence on Independent Television heard the following curious scoreline: Dundee United 0, Portmarnock 1. There is, of course, a famous Scottish football club called *Kil*marnock but if *Port*marnock is famous for anything at all it is a windswept golf course outside Dublin. Had the startled pools-checkers stayed tuned-in for a further minute they would have heard an even more bewildering rugby result. I cannot recollect the two famous teams concerned but one was certainly alleged to have beaten the other 1–0, an outcome not easily achieved under the Rugby Union scoring system.

As the perpetrator of both these gaffes on the first and obviously only occasion I was invited to enlighten the nation about who, roughly, had beaten whom during the afternoon, I am able to reveal that reading the football results is infinitely trickier than it sounds. Certain cadences and

inflections have to be employed in a manner which implies the outcome even before the away team's score is revealed. Summoning a Fleet Street sportswriter to stand in for an indisposed regular results-reader was a stroke of genius comparable to asking the postman to pop in and run up a Cordon Bleu lunch.

Being recruited into television is not necessarily the glamorous career highlight it may seem. Jimmy Hill, then head of sport for an ITV company, chose as his seduction venue a large pub on the road out to Wembley Stadium whose Tudor architecture probably dated back as far as 1953. There were cigarette burns on the table and would have been more on the carpet had there been a carpet. Jimmy's sales pitch was amazing. 'Listen,' he cried, 'don't you want to be *recognized* every morning on your way to the bus stop?' It occurred to me that remaining unrecognized in a Mercedes had greater appeal but joined anyway.

One of our first assignments was to fly down to Australia to make filmed documentaries about Harold Larwood, the great England fast bowler of the bodyline era who had emigrated to Sydney, and an aboriginal girl tennis player as yet unknown in Britain. It was a fascinating insight into the economics and manning levels of Independent Television. While a team of five would have been adequate and six a luxury, various union regulations decreed we were a party of ten. Of these probably five insisted on starting dinner with caviar and ending it with Havana cigars. On the eve of our return the young lady in charge of finances had to request a further £10,000 from London to meet the hotel bill and other incidental expenses incurred in keeping a television crew happy in a five-star corner of a foreign field.

Harold Larwood, forty years earlier, had been the spearhead of Douglas Jardine's ferocious fast-bowling campaign against Australian batsmen in general and Donald

Bradman in particular. I had only seen him on ancient, flickering film, racing in to deliver the 95 mile-an-hour thunderbolts that reared to hit revered heroes on heart and head. At Adelaide a troop of mounted police had to be summoned to guarantee his safety as he left the ground and for some reason I expected to be confronted by a towering Goliath of a man when we arrived at his bungalow on the outskirts of Sydney.

Instead the door was cautiously opened by a tiny grey-haired man, barely 5ft 6in tall, and so meek in manner that I would have re-checked the address had not a strident voice at that moment yelled out: 'Arold, oos that?' Harold Larwood appeared terrified of his wife. Despite the sweltering heat he was wearing a blue serge suit and collar and tie. Rejected by an English cricket establishment which had made him the scapegoat for an acrimonious episode in sport, and wrongly suspecting that the majority of Australians had never forgiven him for the reign of terror he had inflicted on their batsmen, he had virtually shut himself away from the world for the past twenty-five years. It was Mrs Larwood who looked far more likely to have emasculated any opponent who dared stand his ground in her path.

At first Harold was a diffident interviewee on camera but as the days passed his voice grew stronger and his confidence returned as he related for the first time the duplicity of those paternal figures at Lord's, notably Sir Pelham Warner, who had pitched him out with the empties to protect their own careers and reputations.

Our filming required us to prise Harold from his one-storey Dunromin, drive him to locations all over Sydney and reunite him with many of his Australian opponents of forty years before. They did not hate him at all. Bertie Oldfield, whom Larwood had felled into a full night's unconsciousness, greeted him like a brother. The result may not have been the most classic sports documentary ever made but we had the intense satisfaction of knowing that because of it Harold Larwood had returned to the world to spend his remaining years among the friends he mistakenly believed had rejected him.

The second Australian assignment had an equally happy ending. Evonne Goolagong was hardly known in her own State, let alone Britain, when we began filming the warm smile, the lacerating instinctive backhand and the gruelling ten-hours-a-day grooming on court that go into the making of a great tennis champion. The added fascination, clearly, was that not all Australian aboriginals have the chance to make it to the top, however talented.

Evonne, at the time, had already been moved down to a smart tennis ranch in Sydney but, while we were politely discouraged from going there, the essence of the story was back in the red dust and race prejudice of her small home village of Barellan. There was no future in making appointments. We flew to the nearest town, drove out to

towards the endless skyline, swung right and pulled into the yard of a peeling, clapboard house. Mrs Goolagong, soap-sudded to the elbows, was hanging washing on the line.

Would she take us to the wall where Evonne had spent her childhood slamming threadbare balls in endless solo rallies? Better still, would she stand against it and answer a few questions for British television? Evonne's mum clapped a hand resolutely over her mouth. She shook her head. She grimaced. She rolled her eyes. But being Evonne's mum she suddenly dragged her hand away and burst out laughing. 'Just look at me,' she said, revealing naked gums, 'me teeth have gone to Sydney.' There had, apparently, been some mishap with her dentures which had been sent off to the big city for repair. But the Goolagongs have generous hearts and she kindly faced the camera and told us about the early days of the little girl who had suddenly left home.

Later Kenny Goolagong, Evonne's dad, came home and took us to a sheep sale. He was very light-skinned and had with him a cousin who was very dark. We had such an amusing afternoon together that Kenny and cousin drove back with us to the airport. Along the way we called into the bar of the best hotel in Griffith, New South Wales, for a drink. The barman looked at Kenny's cousin and said: 'No abbos.' His patrons stood their ground and said: 'No drink, big trouble.' Reluctantly the drinks were served.

'Thanks,' said Kenny, 'that don't happen too often round here.'

The bad ending was that a few years later Kenny was killed in a car crash. The good ending was that eighteen months after our speculative visit Evonne Goolagong won Wimbledon.

Documentary-making is enduring fun. You point a camera at a place or person, fire off a few questions, take the film back to a dark dungeon known as a cutting room, slash it into short strips, throw most away, assemble what's left into one long strip, write a script that hopefully explains what's going on, read it into a microphone when a green light goes on

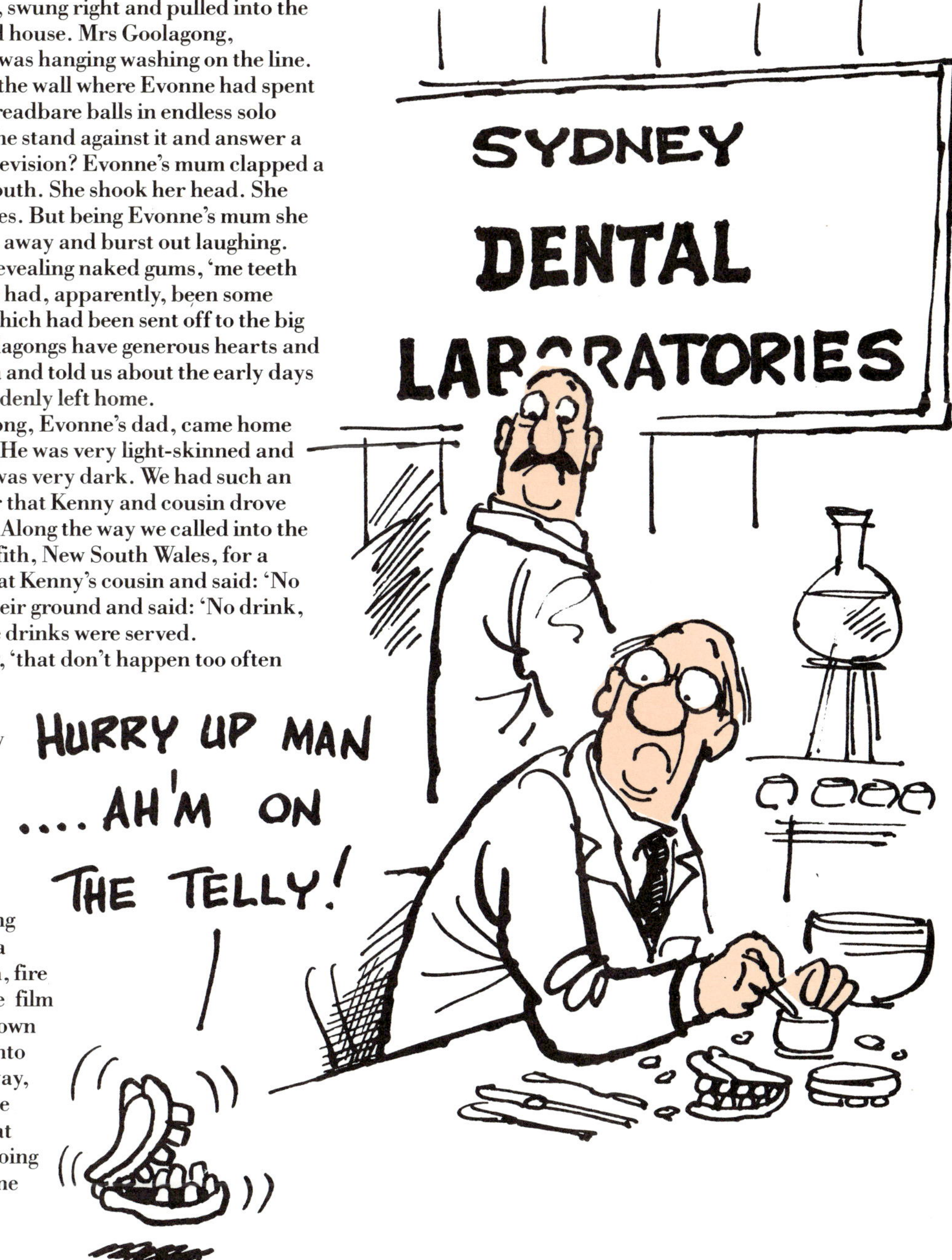

and then wait for the television critics to tear it to pieces again.

All this is very relaxed compared with the live studio television of which men like Frank Bough, Dickie Davies and Harry Carpenter are the supreme masters. Interviewing is comparatively simple, provided you know your subject and concentrate utterly on what your intended victim is saying, but to smile unerringly into-camera and speak coherently while a cacophony of voices is being transmitted to your brain through an earpiece, requires a very special talent.

If you do not have it your pulse-rate doubles about five minutes before transmission and your tongue feels like a piece of scorched sackcloth. You are convinced that when the red light comes on your opening words will sound like the mating croak of some elderly frog. Despite strenuous attempts to convince myself that no-one was watching anyway, I never overcame these manifestations of nerves and said farewell to live studio work without a single backward glance of regret. What precipitated this early retirement was a moment of horror which still recurs in nightmares.

It happened when Colin Welland and I were jointly presenting a live late-evening sports series on BBC Two and it fell to me to introduce an item about the International Olympic Committee and its then president Avery Brundage, a man who became apoplectic about athletes fiddling 60 pence on travelling expenses while his own private collection

of Chinese jade was valued in excess of £30 million.

Since explaining all this was to take a full minute my words were processed for auto-cue, an electronic crib which spools your script down just above the camera lens. If you don't jerk your eyes around you can give the impression you are ad-libbing with conviction but you are, of course, totally at the mercy of the young ladies who operate the machine. If they speed up you gabble. If they slow down you sound as dumb as Alexander Haig. If they stop altogether you stand a good chance of resembling some gulping goldfish.

On the evening of the Brundage story the auto-cue was in the hands of an affectionate girl known to a large circle of close friends as Alley Cat. She had once been swapped by one boy friend to another in a Fleet Street pub in exchange for an expensive bottle of claret.

Alley Cat set out at the perfect speed, and I was priding myself on reading rather well at the very moment some unscheduled words began appearing between the neat lines of typescript. Panic. Was this some important late fact which I was expected to impart to the great British public?

It was just as well I didn't. The little message the lovely Alley Cat had added to my script read: 'This is the most boring ****** programme I've ever had to sit through.'

Another alarming moment came in the tiny studio from which the BBC team operated during the Munich Olympic Games. Wandering around one evening, grubby and

SILENCE. RECORDING
AAAAAAAA

perspiring after a day at the athletics track, I was suddenly dragooned into conducting a live interview with the four members of the British equestrian team who had just won the gold medal. The first embarrassment was that they were already resplendent in gowns and dinner jackets for their up-market evening celebrations. The second was that a day spent watching East German shot-putters and Soviet sprinters was hardly the ideal preparation for interrogating Britain's winning horsepeople.

By royal good luck an expert eyewitness was standing in the cluttered control room waiting to accompany the gold medallists, one of whom was destined to become her husband, to their victory party. Princess Anne's recollection of the vital turning points of the afternoon's proceedings was so lucid and economic in the brief time available that she would make a fine reporter if Britain were ever foolish enough to turn republican.

The briefing was fine but then the luck ran out. The only member of the equestrian team I knew personally was Richard Meade, an ever-calm and articulate man. Why, in those circumstances, I proceeded to address the first question to Captain Mark Phillips I shall never know. The result was total silence. Poor Mark, then completely inexperienced in the ordeal of live television, opened his mouth but not a sound emerged. A silence of probably four seconds at most felt as long as the Grand National. It was broken eventually by Richard Meade who drew the camera to him with a clear and characteristically modest reconstruction of their victory.

Far more amusing was the night Johnny Weissmuller came into the Munich studio to talk about the huge advances in world swimming. Fortunately the man who won five Olympic gold medals in the 1920s and then became the most famous screen Tarzan of them all was appreciably more sober than when I had first approached him in a German restaurant. He spoke admiringly of the phenomenal times Mark Spitz and Shane Gould were achieving in the pool but, surprisingly, seemed reluctant to discuss his career as an actor.

To encourage him I asked him, on the spur of the moment, to perform the famous jungle-call I had heard so many times as a wide-eyed child in the front row of the local cinema. Unfortunately it was a request of which the sound engineers in the neighbouring control room required advance notice.

After two refusals Weissmuller suddenly cupped his hands to his mouth and emitted a mega-decibel shriek so horrendous that small monkeys in Zambia must have fallen

out of trees in fright. More significantly the needles on the sound-control panel next door crashed into the unacceptable zone where they were likely to fall off altogether and across Britain, I gathered later, cut-glass vases and heavy-framed wedding photographs were bouncing around on television sets as though rocked by an earthquake.

In my ignorance of all things electronic I emerged from the studio well pleased at having provoked Tarzan, then 68, into a valedictory rendering of one of the most famous sounds in the history of the cinema. My small triumph was exceedingly short-lived. Paul Fox, now a mogul with Independent Television but then merely the most ferocious boss ever known at the BBC, gave me a withering look and uttered a single word rarely seen in print.

Lord Louis Mountbatten, for all his reputation for imperiousness, was a much more generous man. We were making a documentary film on the months of preparation that still make Trooping the Colour the finest military parade on earth and his eagerness to grant us an interview in his private quarters high up in the tower of the Household Cavalry barracks in Knightsbridge was at first surprising. He greeted us with friendly informality. It could hardly have been otherwise since he was wearing only socks and underpants. His batman and ADC took almost half an hour to dress him and adjust the regalia and decorations of a lifetime's bravery and high office. He then proceeded to direct the BBC's director in precisely how and where he would sit, aware of the exact camera-angle that would show his Romanesque half-profile to best advantage.

'He loves it', whispered his batman. 'At home at Broadlands he often goes to bed at nine o'clock in the evening and watches old films and video tapes of himself.' It was said with great affection, implying pride rather than vanity.

A further astonishing demonstration of this pride was only a few seconds away. To our bewilderment Lord Mountbatten suddenly snapped out the single word 'Wall', using it not as a prosaic noun but as a command. The result made us fear for a moment that his batman and ADC had both suffered brainstorms. They led the great man to the nearest wall, stood him against it, squared up to him with their arms held high and then, simultaneously, slammed the heels of their hands into the fronts of his shoulders with immense force.

No explanation was necessary. Then almost 80, Lord Mountbatten had developed a faint stoop which clearly affronted his dignity. As he stepped away from the wall he was as erect as a 30-year-old guardsman. He then sat bolt upright in a chair, as though posing for a portrait, and spoke faultlessly for twenty minutes of the meaning and emotions of great military pageantry. Courteously he thanked interviewer, director, cameraman and sound-recordist and asked if we would send him a copy of the film.

Tragically he was never to hear the last words he had spoken for television. A few weeks later, working on an athletics story high up in a Montreal hotel, I received a phone call from the *Daily Mail*. 'Give us 600 words on your interview with Lord Mountbatten,' they said. 'Be as quick as you can. The IRA have just blown him to pieces.'

Chapter Eight

BATTING UPSIDE-DOWN

The tidings, across 12,000 miles of radio static, seemed relentlessly disastrous. Australia were always 474 for three with Bradman 227 not out and still accelerating. If England were batting we were usually 125 for six. Actually the record books do not substantiate those childhood recollections but the scene itself remains clear enough: a small boy, huddled in a thick dressing-gown against the winter cold, ear glued to a fretwork-cased wireless driven by wet and dry batteries, dotting every run and ball of the first post-war Test matches in Melbourne, Adelaide and Sydney. Sheer distance, time-difference and the bewilderment that Bradman was batting upside-down all heightened the drama of those early-morning vigils. Anyway, it was by the grey ashes of an English fireside that a lifelong love affair with Australia began. The sun always seemed to shine there and the voices were full of vigour and self-assurance. I even tried an Australian accent for half a term, abandoning it only when it

HOWDO
SHEILA!

was clearly making no impression on the pubescent girls of Form 3b.

It was to be a further sixteen years before I got there, not in the gold and scarlet braided blazer of an England cricketer but as a sportswriter. Only the great Sir Donald Bradman was a disappointment. He had little of the warmth of Australia about him and seemed to be calculating the fiscal value of every sentence he reluctantly uttered. A few English cricket correspondents got along with him famously. My distant relationship became utterly extinct when I later wrote the story of how his son, John, exhausted by living in the shadow of a paternal genius, changed his surname by deed-poll to Bradsen. The Don never spoke to me again or even glanced in my direction.

It was my loss, not his, I realize, for his was the most formidable brain ever to be applied to cricket. Only one opposing captain ever really rattled him and that was Douglas Jardine, a Wykehamist who regarded all Australians as unspeakable cads. As England's captain in Australia in the notorious campaign of 1932–33, he napalmed the opposition with the bodyline bowling which not only won the Ashes but reduced Bradman's batting average to artisan dimensions. Bradman never forgot it, at least not for twenty-six years. In 1958, when Jardine died, a reporter approached Sir Donald and asked him for a few sentences by way of tribute to a fallen opponent. 'No comment,' replied probably the best batsman and worst loser who ever lived.

If I write with less than fervour of Bradman it is because I saw him as such a bleak contrast to the scores of instantly friendly and relentlessly generous Australians met on eight visits to that vibrant society.

To see the great cricket arenas of the childhood imagination was to discover that all the lies were true. Sydney, with its green turreted pavilions, really *was* a cathedral of the game. Melbourne's enormous concrete bowl, with room for 120,000, really *did* terrify visiting batsmen, however battle-hardened they professed to be.

Few came more resilient than the late Ken Barrington yet even he, during the turmoils of a Test Match, tossed and turned at night. I was amazed, returning to Melbourne's Windsor Hotel in the early hours of a Test Match morning, to discover him sitting alone in the vast lounge contemplating a glass of whisky but spectacularly sober. It was the more surprising because he was a not-out batsman overnight, carried most of England's hopes later that morning and was a man of extreme self-discipline and meticulous preparation.

'Can't sleep,' moaned Ken. 'Went to bed at ten absolutely knackered. Thrashed about for hours. Still wide awake so I came down here.' We had a commiserative drink together before Ken returned to his room. An hour later, still fast awake, he took the ultimate desperate measure of lifting the house phone and asking to be connected to the Duke of Norfolk, the aforementioned team manager. The Duke, a celebrated near-insomniac himself who relied on heavy sedative bombs to get a good night's rest, was less than pleased at being so abruptly woken.

When he finally grasped Barrington's predicament and its possible bearing on the result of a Test Match he said: 'All right, you may have a couple of my pills if you come and get them now.'

Barrington replaced the telephone, fell back on his pillow and instantly went to sleep. The Duke waited. He waited until dawn, then rose and staggered to the breakfast table. 'Damn you, Barrington,' are reputed to be the only words he uttered but I doubt them. England won the match by seven wickets.

Mercifully the incident never reached the ears of the Australian Press, whose ranks at the time appeared to include a number of graduates from the Paul Joseph Goebbels School of Journalism. Their genius for manufacturing virulent anti-Pom propaganda out of the hot-air was revealed on the newspaper placards that confronted that same MCC team on their very first afternoon after landfall in Perth. On their passage through the Indian Ocean they had been approached by Gordon Pirie, the British runner who was travelling steerage on the same liner, with an offer to train them to a new pinnacle of physical fitness.

The fitness required of a 5,000-metre Olympic athlete bears no relation, of course, to the ox-like stamina needed to survive a five-day Test Match. Fast bowlers, particularly, have re-charged their batteries with beer ever since the game was invented, a fact which Pirie either never knew or chose to ignore. As the Australian Pressmen boarded the *Canberra* for the traditional arrival interviews, Pirie cornered one of them and sold him an exclusive story claiming the England team to be alarmingly unfit as a result of their long days and nights in the bar.

This dramatic scoop was soon rolling off the presses. Hundreds of newspaper bills proclaimed: 'English Team on Drink Charge'.

There was no real cause for alarm. It was an old Australian technique, seen at its best when a famous

Queensland Rugby League player named Pope sustained a minor muscular injury a few days before an important match. An enterprising newspaper circulation manager immediately flooded a predominantly Catholic suburb of Brisbane with placards reading: 'Grave Bulletin on Pope'.

Pom-baiting is one of Australia's favourite national sports. The only known antidote is good-humoured counter-attack. This requires straight-faced assertions of the nature that the acoustics of the Sydney Opera House make it the best indoor cycle-speedway stadium in the world, Joan Sutherland is earning quite a name for herself in British music hall and that you have never heard of films called *Gallipoli*, *Breaker Morant* or *Picnic at Hanging Rock*.

One story guaranteed to silence any intellectual Australian dinner table is strictly accurate. During the construction of a BBC television documentary called *Mr Packer and the Poms*, a profile of the much-abused Australian TV and publishing tycoon and his cataclysmic disruption of established world cricket, we decided to ask the actor Barry Humphries to play his celebrated role as Sir Les Patterson, Australia's mythical cultural attaché in London, in a filmed interview over a working lunch. The idea, obviously, was to prick the sheer pomposity of those who would cheerfully have seen Kerry Packer hung at Tyburn and drawn, quartered and sold for dog meat down the road at Harrods.

The sequence was filmed in a private dining-room in the Old Ship Hotel at Brighton, close by the theatre where Humphries was currently appearing. He tore through the door in the emotionally-charged state he clearly has to generate to produce his finest work. He already *was* Sir Les Patterson, snorting, hawking, spitting, swearing, blaspheming, slopping five-fingers of whisky in the rough direction of his glass before spilling much of the rest down his appalling Mafia suit and the scarf-wide tie with the kangaroo motif. Throughout lunch he answered questions with outrageous gusto while cascading good claret down his shirt, stuffing steak, spaghetti and avocado pear into his mouth simultaneously and smearing leaking gravy across his face with the back of a hand already holding a lighted cigarette. 'That Kerry Packer,' concluded Sir Les after a salvo of horrendous belches, 'is a right good Okker, my word he is.'

That the Barry Humphries sequence caused grave offence to a number of administrators who regard cricket as a private religion was hardly surprising. Nor did it matter. Packer, although few could see it at the time, grabbed a professional sport off its deathbed and dragged it screaming into an era when, like it or not, only the most professionally-run sports can hope to survive. Nor, at a personal level, is he the stocking-masked ogre portrayed by his determined opponents in the broadsheet British Press. He has many graces, not least intense loyalty to his friends and the strength to tell unpalatable truths when others would protect their popularity with lies.

But I digress. It would not be the mention of Kerry Packer that would demolish the Australian dinner table. It would be the relevation that for days after the documentary was screened we were bombarded with phone calls and letters from viewers who never realized that the Barry Humphries-Sir Les Patterson interview was a leg-pull.

A dozen times I was asked: 'How did that frightful man ever become a *cultural attaché?*' Or: 'Do *many* Australians carry on like that?' Many hundreds, it transpired, switched off convinced that Sir Leslie Patterson was the genuine article, a dinkum Australian diplomat with responsibility for that nation's burgeoning interest in the fine arts. In some cases I didn't bother to disabuse them.

Fortunately, like most people who regard 'Hello, you old bastard' as a formal mode of address, most Australian sportsmen can withstand criticism and accept a joke. I believe I have been as critical as any sportswriter of the more excessive lapses in behaviour of Ian Chappell and Dennis Lillee yet it has never impaired our personal relationships. They are firebrands but they do not cheat, and away from the stress of intense competition they are engaging and generous companions.

The relationship that *was* fragile for a while was with Jeff Thomson, who emerged almost overnight in 1974 as the world's fastest bowler. His arrival in England coincided with an idea I had to produce a mythical character called Terror Tomkins, a Pommie-bashing Australian cricketer whose letters back home to his mother became the subjects of several of my *Daily Mail* columns. Terror's dad was invariably in the nick, his girl-friend usually pregnant. His prose style matched his dreadful spelling and his malapropisms were prodigious. It was a device, of course, to make observations that could not be made in a conventional column and to retaliate a little, perhaps, for the fearful punishment that the Australian Sporting Press had inflicted on English cricketers down the years.

Unfortunately I chose in the initial column to describe Terror Tomkins as a fast bowler. This, plus the similarity in surname and a beautifully drawn caricature by the artist Michael Frith, which did bear some mild resemblance to

VATICAN NEWS
POPE LATEST

FLYING DOCTOR

Australia's sudden pace-bowling discovery, convinced Jeff Thomson that he was the subject of some pernicious Fleet Street send-up. There was talk of legal action but fortunately the wise counsel of a mutual friend prevailed and an amusing and probably horrendously expensive court action was avoided. The truth, anyway, was that at that stage I had never exchanged a word with Thomson and Frith had never set eyes on him.

Terror was to remain an occasional *Daily Mail* 'contributor' for the next five years, commenting on anything from the sexual mores of well-born ladies in Knightsbridge to the syntax of British Leyland's shop stewards. Many were reprinted in Australian newspapers as if they were a send-up of some of the more eccentric figures in British life.

In 1980 there was a delightful sequel. Jeff Thomson, working in conjunction with David Frith, a meticulous and respected cricket biographer, published his life story. He quoted the Tomkins Letters extensively and could not have been more magnanimous in acknowledging that he had enjoyed the spurious notoriety they had brought him. All, apparently, was forgiven.

Australia, with its pride and independence, remains a rich hunting-ground for the reporter. It is as alive with character as Runyon's Broadway. My hero among all the heroes never played for his country at any sport yet he epitomized the spirit that down the years has made Australia so hard to beat in the arena. He was a 60-year-old Sydney man who took his crippling arthritis to the doctor and was told his condition was incurable. 'I'm afraid,' said the doctor, 'that you'll just have to resign yourself to living the last years of your life in a wheelchair.'

Nothing was heard of the man for more than three years. Then one morning a local journalist bothered to talk to an unshaven figure who was briskly pushing a home-made hand-cart down the main street of a small town between Melbourne and Sydney. An epic story emerged. The old boy had defeated the doctor's diagnosis by *walking* 12,000 miles around the outside of Australia. Asked by a television interviewer why he had done it he produced an immortal line. 'Well, mate,' he said, 'y' just had to beat the bastard.'

Another iconoclast who has devoted many years to helping Australia's sports stars 'beat the bastards' is Dr Brian Corrigan, whose occasionally baroque behaviour tends to conceal the fact that he is one of the world's leading authorities in sports medicine. Many of his country's cricketers, footballers and Olympic athletes owe their fame to his down-to-earth advice and attention. Characteristically he prefers to regale lunch tables with his more memorable disasters, the most notable of which occurred in Mexico City even before the 1968 Olympic Games had started.

To combat the growing boredom among the waiting Australian contingent he arranged to take a large party to the Sunday bull-fights. Among them were tiny girl swimmers who hardly knew the facts of life and young country lads to whom sophistication until then had meant a day out at a sheep-shearing competition. Even Corrigan was mildly apprehensive when he discovered that their tickets for Mexico's awesome bullring placed them in the *contra-barrera*, the equivalent of the second row in the stalls and thus somewhat close to the gory rituals of tauromachy for those of a sensitive disposition. His concern was not unjustified.

The very first matador elected to open the *corrida* with one of the most dangerous gambits in the repertoire of passes. He knelt twenty yards from the door from which the bull was imminently to charge, spread his cape in front of him and waited motionless. It is one of the most glorious movements in bull-fighting when executed perfectly: the matador rises, whirls the cape around him in a magenta cloud and the beautiful animal, as yet undamaged by the vicious picadors, explodes into what proves to be the mirage of his enemy.

Unfortunately the Mexican bullfighter was fractionally slow to rise. The cape was not yet swinging when the bull gored him through the centre of his chest. Death in the afternoon suddenly assumed a different meaning as the bull ran free and Australia's tyro Olympians found themselves staring in horror at a corpse. It was not the ideal distraction, perhaps, for those about to take part in far less pagan competition but Dr Corrigan's pupils eventually recovered to storm away with five gold, seven silver and five bronze medals.

Corrigan's even greater coup, however, was to come some years later when his close friend Richie Benaud, rated by Australia's opponents as the shrewdest of all Test captains, boarded a plane in Sydney to come to England for another summer's BBC television commentating. Despite being a man whose multiple business interests impel him to use the world's airways like most people commute on buses, Benaud has never conquered a deep-rooted fear of flying. When he asks for a large drink before the plane has taxied out from the boarding ramp it is strictly for medicinal reasons. Even then a few more double measures of liquid reassurance are required before he can relax and sleep.

On this occasion his invariably polite request for a stiff dry martini was refused. More curiously still, since he knows most airline stewards by their Christian names, his second request immediately the seat-belts were unfastened was also greeted by embarrassed head-shaking. Apocolypse right now occurred when the drinks trolley finally arrived and, at the third time of asking, he was firmly refused a drink. 'Sorry, Mr Benaud,' apologized the steward, 'but I'm afraid we have instructions not to serve you with alcohol on this entire flight.'

Mr Benaud, when roused, is the only man I know who can sound like Edward Carson without even moving his lips. 'Would you kindly present my compliments to the captain,' he said, 'and ask him if he could spare me a moment when it appears likely that this plane is reasonably safe from mid-air disintegration?'

The captain was not long in arriving. 'Look, Richie,' he whispered, 'you know I wouldn't do this to you but, you see, we got this letter. . . .'

'Letter?' demanded Benaud. 'What letter?'

'Well, as a matter of fact,' replied the captain, 'it's from a doctor. To be perfectly frank what it says is that under no circumstances must we serve you with . . . .'

'There's no chance, I suppose,' interrupted Benaud, 'that it's signed by a chap I used to know named Corrigan?'

Well, that's Australia.

Chapter Nine

WAITING FOR N'GODU

A constant source of entertainment down the years has been the intrusion of politics into sport. Many people are outraged that almost no major sporting event can be staged these days without someone wanting to ban it, bomb it or boycott it. Mostly these people own minimally six suits, four bedrooms and two cars and thus tend to overlook the fact that South Africa's blacks don't appreciate being treated like cattle, Afghanistans dislike being shot at by Russians and that Jews and Arabs will never hit it off. Since global sporting events attract global television, and outrageous acts of global TV are the only means by which militant minorities can attract attention to themselves and their causes, I am afraid we must all resign ourselves to the fact that the Olympic Games and the World Cup, to name but two, are but in the infancy of their political disruption.

Some sportswriters, mostly of the older school, tend deliberately to ignore political intrusion. Some fail to understand it. There is a famous story, of the Rugby League correspondent of a leading national Sunday newspaper who was travelling to Australia with the British team at the height of the Aden troubles.

Their plane landed for a night's stop-over at Aden and amid the sounds of appalling explosions from the Crater District, where Colonel Colin 'Mad' Mitchell was leading a retaliatory action against some nasty natives who definitely deserved it, the players and reporters drove to their hotel and made straight for the bar. Glasses bounced on tables and the air was full of cordite. The telephone rang. It was a call from the Sunday newspaper's Manchester office for their intrepid correspondent.

'Thank God we've got you,' cried the voice from Manchester. 'Listen, we're putting you straight over to copy. Just give us the facts. We'll tidy it up here.'

In newspaper parlance 'putting you over to copy' is the act of switching the reporter over to a typist who will take down his words. By this enormous stoke of luck the Sunday newspaper had an on-the-spot witness to one of the last *Boys' Own Paper* actions in the history of the British Empire. Hold the front page!

In Manchester, rejoicing at the scoop to come, editor, assistant editors and sub-editors rushed in to stand at the shoulder of the typist hammering down the words by phone from Aden. Re-write men were standing by to transform the hastily dictated impressions of violent battle into crisp, dramatic English.

They were slightly perturbed by the words they saw appearing. They read:

'Aden, Saturday. John Smith' – I invent the name for obvious reasons – 'is doubtful for First Test in Australia. A hamstring injury sustained when . . . .'

It can happen to us all. It happened to me on an innocent morning in Madrid. The previous evening I had attended a European Cup football match and was sitting in the bar of the Palace Hotel with the ebullient Lord Hesketh, then in his mid-twenties, probably weighing eighteen stone, positively managing the young James Hunt's motor-racing career and definitely interested in vodka. We were on our fourth large one of the morning when there was an abrupt summons to the telephone. The voice from London was that of Brian Freemantle, now a fine espionage-thriller author but then foreign editor of the *Daily Mail*. We were mates from way-back but the tone was professionally curt. 'Get a car *now*,' he ordered, 'and get to Lisbon *fast*. They're shutting the frontiers and you're the nearest man we've got.'

The Portuguese revolution had started.

Back in the bar it was a surprise to discover that Alexander Hesketh, usually portrayed in the gossip columns as a portly playboy without a brain in his head, had just read General Spinola's book advocating urgent social reform for Portugal. Now, across the border, Spinola was implementing his ideas at gunpoint while in Madrid Hesketh was swiftly briefing the *Daily Mail*'s newest foreign correspondent.

Revolutions, kick-off times unknown, no Press boxes for privileged vantage points, are far more fun than football games, particularly when the bloodshed is minimal. There were only nine deaths in the first week of the coup and with the young officers sporting carnations in every buttonhole and the citizens rejoicing nightly in the streets, the scene was straight from the first act of some bouncy operetta.

Four of us shared a car in the dash from Madrid. They included the distinguished correspondent of one of Britain's more serious publications who drank brandy all the way and reassured us that nothing that lay ahead could conceivably match the horror of his latest domestic mishap. While consoling his latest girl-friend in the reverse missionary position, his pet monkey, consumed by jealousy, had leaped from the top of the wardrobe and landed four-square on the lady's back. She had run screaming from the apartment, not even waiting to gather up her more fundamental garments.

'Absolute hell to pay, old boy,' said the correspondent. 'Rather glad to get away as a matter of fact.'

Ten miles inside Portugal we passed the army column moving up to seal the border. In Lisbon some scared-looking boy soldiers in gas capes forgot to search our car for weapons and politely directed us to General Spinola's villa headquarters. Words of description, if not exactly wisdom, were filed to London. The greater problem was what to do for cash. The banks were shut, credit cards were not being honoured and funds were critically low.

Cockney resource again came to the rescue. The nephew of the *Daily Mail*'s doyen photographer Monty Fresco, a *Daily Mirror* cameraman confusingly called Monte Fresco, discovered that it required more than a mere revolution to persuade the nearby Estoril Casino to stop trading. We pooled our meagre resources and with £70 between us caught the train out to the beautiful gaming house by the sea. Nothing concentrates the mind like the spectre of bankruptcy. On one roulette table Fresco played the even chances with bravado and frequent thumbs-up signs. On another my own illogical affection for the numbers 7, 17 and 27 for once paid off. We caught a taxi back to Lisbon, funded for a week.

Total ignorance of the etiquette of revolution-coverage proved no hindrance. Instead of attending the official daily Press briefings we befriended the young naval officers who had occupied the headquarters of PIDE, the hated Portuguese secret police. They showed us confidential files, offered us sub-machine guns as souvenirs, took us into an amazing room in which the seedy PIDE agents had assembled what must have been the biggest cache of pornography in Europe, and fed us with sufficient human-interest stories to fill two pages of our newspapers daily. Eventually the frontiers were opened and the officially-accredited foreign correspondents arrived, frowning slightly at our impudent presence. We departed sadly. Spurs v Manchester United was a definite anti-climax.

Occasionally, however, even sports reporting has its moments of mild excitement, none more so for me than in the early light of a Sunday morning on a bleak stretch of the six-lane highway that runs south from Los Angeles to the

Mexican border. Overnight we had watched Jim Ryun attempt to smash the world indoor-mile record and were heading to spend a few days with Billy Casper, the Mormon golfer, at his home in Chula Vista. Normally I refrain from mentioning any sportsman's religion or lack of it, but the significance of it in Casper's case will become alarmingly apparent.

Phil Pilley, then a BBC producer, was stretched out asleep across the back seat. Patricia Smith, his assistant, was dozing in the front. It was my turn to drive and since there was no traffic, the road was dry and the car effortlessly powerful, a steady 90mph seemed reasonable for all concerned. Unfortunately it was not reasonable at all to the police officer driving the black highway-patrol car that suddenly appeared from nowhere in the rear-view mirror.

Easing back to 60mph, ignoring the light blazing on the patrol car's roof, convinced that Californian policemen are reasonable chaps, I drove on for a further two miles before a sudden blast of siren implied that our pursuer was intent on conversation. We swung over to the hard-shoulder and stopped. The patrol car stopped 30 yards behind. Phil Pilley, awake now, imparted some disturbing information. 'For God's sake,' he said, 'he's got a gun.'

Far from merely *having* a gun, the young patrolman was actually *aiming* it at the left-hand door of our car. He had a thin, pale face and was crouched, legs splayed, in a manner I had only previously seen in *Kojak* films. He looked dangerously nervous. 'Throw out the keys,' he shouted.

Unfortunately this was more easily ordered than accomplished. In my panic to comply with anything this apparently lunatic cop requested I accidentally nudged the steering wheel and locked the keys into the ignition. I shall never know how long it took to extricate them – probably five seconds at most – but it was long enough to feel the sweat of true fear running down the back of a head which seemed likely to have a large hole in it if I didn't hurry. Eventually the keys came clear and I tossed them out the window.

'Get out, put your hands in the air and walk backwards on to this gun,' was the next command. Too scared to appreciate the absurdity of this nightmare in the Californian dawn I walked backwards, hands aloft, until they were jerked downwards and handcuffed behind my back in one swift movement. Then, with the gun pressing on some middle vertebra, I was shoved forward again and made to lay prostrate over the boot of the car. Phil Pilley was then subjected to exactly the same treatment. Miss Smith was simply told to get out and stand absolutely still in the dusty verge.

By now a second patrol car had arrived at the scene of a minor traffic offence. The next voice to speak was much deeper and more mature. 'Turn around,' it said. We turned and faced a rifle. It was held by a man who looked as though he had four children, two grandchildren and thoughts of imminent retirement. 'Yer resistin' arrest,' he said enigmatically to two men trussed like oven-ready turkeys.

I do not remember who spoke first but the English accent helped. The manic apprentice removed our handcuffs while the older man explained that a blazing light on an American patrol car is the signal to stop for questioning and that to fail to do so, particularly when you are heading for Mexico with your foot down, amounts to an act of singular folly. 'We had eighteen policemen killed on the roads of California last year,' he said, 'and we don't take no chances.'

He regaled us with a fascinating postscript. A few weeks earlier a deaf-mute had been stopped for a traffic misdemeanour on the outskirts of Los Angeles. Impulsively he reached into an inside jacket pocket for some identification document. The bullet hit him in the stomach and he died some hours later in hospital.

Badly shaken, we drove onwards to Chula Vista. Never had a large, strong drink been less contra-indicated but, of course, at 9 am the bars were shut. Billy Casper greeted us with the reminder that the Mormon faith proscribed even tea and coffee. Alcohol was therefore on a par with LSD. Our work that day, I fear, did not go well.

Getting arrested is from time to time inevitable in countries which do not share Britain's tolerant attitudes to Press comment. To write in London that Margaret Thatcher speaks like a parakeet which once flew over Roedean is

undeniably rude but it is not an indictable offence. Elsewhere presidents and prime ministers tend to be more sensitive, nowhere more so than in Zaire, the former Belgian Congo.

In an earlier chapter I lamented the chaotic communications system that awaited the hundreds of sportswriters who arrived there to cover the epic fight between Muhammad Ali and George Foreman. Nightly we had to make an eighty-mile round journey from the fighters' camp into the capital, Kinshasa, for the privilege of bribing and counter-bribing the world's worst telex operators to transmit our dispatches to Fleet Street. The extortion terms soon became so monstrous that one evening, spotting an operator slide out to the lavatory, I borrowed his keyboard and began tapping out to London a somewhat less-than-flattering description of this fledgling African state and its less-than-adequate ruler whom I referred to by his pre-independence name of Joseph Mobutu. Admittedly this was impolite to a gentleman who now chose to call himself Mobutu Sese Seko Kuku Ngbendu Wa Za Banga but, in the circumstances, Joseph or even Joe struck me as being quite sufficient.

This view was not shared by the zealous army officer who had silently postioned himself behind me to read the glowing account of his nation's culture that this foreign reporter was presumably filing to his British readers. Clearly he was not impressed. A black arm suddenly speared past my right shoulder and ripped the copy from the machine. As I had been transmitting live to the *Daily Mail*, the five paragraphs I had managed to hack out in the time it takes a Zaire telex operator to relieve himself were already in my office. But there were to be no more words that night.

Two expressionless members of the Zaire army's other ranks were summoned to frog-march me to the nearest lift and into the chilling presence of a Mr N'Godu, whose function was less clear than his hostility. He wore what appeared to be an elaborately embroidered nightgown and spoke English so impeccably that he could only have acquired his accent at considerable expense to the British taxpayer. We did not see eye to eye from the start though this concerned me considerably less than the fact that Mr N'Godu had locked his door and removed the key before making a number of phone calls in a language in which the only word I could understand was my surname.

Over the next two hours my host affected to busy himself with affairs of state, pausing occasionally to re-read my offending cable. Eventually the telephone rang. Mr

N'Godu said nothing. He replaced the receiver. 'You are guilty,' he announced, 'of undesirable writing.' He walked to the door, unlocked it and gestured me out. Outside three British journalists were waiting. In turn my Fleet Street colleagues had picketed Mr N'Godu's door. It is a good club to belong to.

What you learn from such an incident is that colonial rule will not be forgiven overnight. Even in Barbados, the most welcoming of the Caribbean islands, you can find yourself in trouble for disseminating the most truthful and innocent observations.

More by way of homage than to conduct an interview, I went to visit the mother of Sir Garfield Sobers, supreme cricketer and a long-time friend, at her tiny, stilted home on the outskirts of Bridgetown. Her frailty belied the enormous strength of a woman who had reared her self-willed sons in widowhood after her husband had been drowned in the Atlantic while serving Britain in World War II.

Writing later of our long and enchanting talk I mentioned that there were holes in the wooden floor of her home through which you could peer down on the profusion of tropical flowers beneath. They weren't very *large* holes but holes they definitely were. My reference to them in no way implied slatternly housekeeping on the part of a charming elderly lady or filial neglect by Garfield. Had her son bought her an air-conditioned apartment on the fashionable St James's coast it is certain that his mother would have chosen not to move there away from her lifelong friends.

My interview was duly published in the *Daily Mail* and I thought no more of it until some mornings later when I drove into the Barbados Test Match ground and was intrigued by a group of probably twenty demonstrators making agitated noises and brandishing placards. One read: 'Expel this Racist'. It came as a disturbing surprise to discover that the alleged racist in question was none other than me. An article in the Barbados newspaper, filed from London, claimed that I had not only insulted the mother of their great sporting hero but subjected the whole island to ridicule. This was distinctly not the case but try explaining that to a bunch of yobs determined to hold you personally responsible for initiating the slave trade. There was some jostling but no blows were struck and happily by the following day the demonstrators had found another target.

If arrest is unavoidable I do recommend the Royal Canadian Mounted Police, particularly if you haven't jeopardized their proud record of always getting their man.

WHO ARE THOSE PEOPLE WITH IAN WOOLDRIDGE ?

In my case this wasn't difficult since two inspectors first telephoned my hotel room in Edmonton and came round, somewhat disappointingly in civilian clothes, by appointment. At first they were rather stern and I suppose this was understandable.

The cause for their concern had its roots in a friendship struck up two years earlier at the Montreal Olympic Games with Joel Bonn, an official of the newest, smallest and happiest member-nation of the Olympic family, the Cayman Islands. Their entire competitive contingent of one, and the men who appointed themselves to oversee his training, epitomized the true spirit of the Games. They gave parties, outrageously amusing interviews and went round sticking Cayman Islands badge-pins into the lapels of bemused Russians and East Germans. The grim politically-harrassed Olympics sorely needs the light relief they provided and it was a delight to meet up with them again two years later at the Commonwealth Games in Edmonton.

By now they were big-time, having brought three boxers and a 10,000-metre runner. 'Listen,' said Joel Bonn, 'you were the guy who discovered us in Montreal, why don't you join our team as an official? We'll make you Chief of Protocol or something like that and then you can sit in on all the meetings and really learn what's going on.'

Sitting in on meetings had little appeal. What had enormous appeal was the fact that if I became a Cayman Islands official I could march with their team in the opening ceremony, an experience offered to few sportswriters of uncertain years and too much weight.

Already accredited as a journalist, I was taken off by Bonn to be accredited again as the Cayman Islands protocol chief. Amazingly, in view of the intense security-screening, this was granted at the mere drop of the request.

The march around the roaring arena, the smart eyes-right to the Queen and Prince Philip, aroused emotions that weren't hard to write about. Unfortunately they were also written about at considerable length in a Canadian newspaper which pointed out in strong terms that if a British reporter could breach the Mounties' security cordon as easily as that, so could an IRA gunman, a PLO terrorist or any psychotic seeking a place in history.

The Royal Canadian Mounted Police were not amused. They discussed a number of charges but then, as the sun went down and a bottle of duty-free Chivas Regal was opened, they tended to relax. Two hours later we were all very relaxed indeed. The Mounties are top cops in my book, but how they stay on those horses I shall never know.

As retired Chief of Protocol for the Cayman Islands it behoves me to record how our athletes fared in those Commonwealth Games. Well, our first boxer almost survived the first round of his first contest before being knocked out. Our second boxer copped it in round two. Our third confirmed an enormous potential by only losing on points. The enigma at the time was our 10,000-metres star of whom great things, such as 20th place, were anticipated. Alas, the lad staggered in last-but-one, a setback for the form book which was not explained for some days.

In true Cayman Island tradition he had honourably proposed marriage to an extremely attractive girl on the very eve of the race. Naturally she accepted. I do not presume to guess at what hour the celebration of this happy contract ended, but it's fair to say that our hero deserved a specially-struck gold medal for finishing at all.

Chapter Ten

SEVENTY-ONE BEDS PER ANNUM

There are mornings when you wake up and cannot believe they pay you for it. By nightfall you will have seen another Test Match day in Sydney or Port of Spain, a Grand Prix in Brazil or Monaco, a world heavyweight title fight in Las Vegas or darkest Africa, a tennis match in Wimbledon or Melbourne, a wrestling contest in Tokyo, a chess think-in in Iceland, the 100-metres or 1,500-metres Olympic finals in Rome or Moscow or maybe just the Cup Final at Wembley. It adds up, in a good year, to about 150,000 miles, 70 hotels, 3,500 telephone calls and between 200,000 and 210,000 words. There are times, struggling with the words, when you would cheerfully chuck it all for some quiet index-linked pension life at the Ministry of Anything but it is surprising how swiftly a good dinner at the Algonquin in New York or the Peninsula, Hong Kong, will bring you to your senses.

The Peninsula management send an olive-green Rolls Royce to meet you at the airport. Two minutes after you

reach your room a servant enters bearing a tray and invites you to choose from any of the world's dozen most luxurious toilet soaps. An expansive friend of mine from the *Daily Express* said: 'Yes, that will do very nicely, thank you.' He grabbed the tray and hurled all twelve soaps into his case. You meet all kinds of people and learn many recondite things along the sportswriting road.

You learn that jet propulsion, motorways, six-hour laundries, penicillin, plastic credit cards, secretaries who can actually write shorthand, and whisky are the seven real wonders of the world. The whisky is to brush your teeth with in India where some taps drip pure hemlock. You learn the truth of a phrase that Cliff Michelmore once coined or quoted: take half the clothes and twice the money. You learn to cram suits, shirts and shoes into your hand-baggage to save hanging around at airports. You learn to eat only one meal in three on long-haul trips to Australia to prevent feeling like death when you get off. You learn, if you are right-handed and propose to work on the plane, to choose a right-hand window seat. If you don't your neighbour, however well bred, will inhibit you by glancing at your last sentence. You learn that first-class airline travel is frequently

a waste of your money or your firm's. The free champagne comes quite expensive when, quite often, you could stretch out across three seats back in tourist class and gĕt a good night's sleep. You learn that jet-lag is a term invented by second-division salesmen who come home with an empty order-book. What you do on arrival is adjust your watch to local time, carry on and go to bed as usual. You learn when travelling between Britain and the United States to fly Concorde on every occasion you can induce someone else to pay the fare.

For a lark we once used Concorde for an unusual golf match. On the eve of New Year's Eve, and thus on almost the shortest day of the year, we played the first nine holes at Royal Mid-Surrey, took a taxi to London Airport, recharged our batteries with Dom Perignon '69 on the 3,778-mile, 3-hour 56-minute crossing to Washington on Concorde Alpha Delta, drove out past the Pentagon to the Army and Navy Country Club and there played the second nine holes. The five-hour time-difference allowed us to complete the contest in a single span of daylight. In the bar that evening we met an American lady of indeterminate age, much plastic surgery and several marriages, the latest of which apparently allowed

her to call herself the Countess von Essen. 'How have you spent your day?' inquired the Countess. 'Playing golf', we replied. 'Oh,' huffed the lady, 'how stupendously boring.'

On the homeward journey, 2,000 miles out over the Atlantic and at an altitude almost twice the height of Mount Everest, my opponent, Trevor Nash, struck an undeviating putt down the aisle of Concorde into a wine glass. Since the plane was travelling at 1,400 miles an hour at the time, the flight-deck computer soon calculated that the putt had actually travelled 5,111 feet, a distance from which even the great Jack Nicklaus has occasionally been known to miss. What was even more stupendously boring was that the *Guinness Book of Records* subsequently refused to deem it worthy of inclusion.

Thankfully the *Daily Mail* has a long track-record of encouraging its reporters to renounce the comforts of a Press box and join in. One of the more esoteric discoveries of my sports editor, Tom Clarke, was a 1,110-mile sled-dog race across the same outer wastes of Alaska that eighty years previously had claimed the lives of hundreds of ill-fed and wrongly-clothed men in their avaricious rush for gold.

It was a sleepy Sunday evening when Clarke

telephoned and inquired: 'How are you feeling, baby?' This solicitous approach invariably means you can cancel all engagements for the next fortnight. In this case it was almost a month. A few days later photographer Monty Fresco and I were flying low along the Iditarod Trail that winds out west from Anchorage, crosses the broken molars of the Alaska Range, swoops down to the Yukon, turns up the Norton Sound and ends in Nome, a wild town that stares straight up the wrong end of Siberia. An equivalent distance is from London to Naples but the analogy is a bad one. It implies warmth and civilization, both of which are conspicuous by their absence through the Eskimo and Indian territories of Jack London's old Alaska.

Below us, padding onwards at eight miles an hour and 5,000 canine strides to the mile, the huskies were dragging their mushers on what the *Daily Mail* was billing as The Last Great Race on Earth. It was, too, but the real race was to find somewhere to sleep. Delusions of comfort disappeared first night out. Fresco's ingenuity found us a double bed-frame in a log cabin which, by 4 am, was occupied by 28 mushers who came in stamping snow from their feet and thus contributing to the inch-deep pool of water on the floor. This we fell into when the bed broke. On a corner stove the mushers were boiling up huge chunks of horse flesh to feed to their dogs for breakfast. The cabin was so blue with fetid fumes that you could almost cut solid cubes of the atmosphere to keep as grisly souvenirs. No dawn would have ever been more beautiful had the temperature outside not been 45° Fahrenheit below. This dropped to 80° below on the unsheltered side of the Alaska Range when the cruel winds off Siberia brought the chill factor into play. On a soft European face it felt as though the skin was being scoured right down to the nerve ends with steel wool.

Our bush pilot, Serge Amundson, flew us up four valleys of the Alaska Range before he finally lifted his 31-year-old Piper aircraft clear of the swirling cloud and got us to the other side. We were luckier than the Spanish television crew who came to film the race two years later, struck a mountain face and died.

The huskies are the heroes. They have indomitable hearts and will run on till they drop. The Iditarod that year was won by 800 yards in 16 hours 27 minutes and 13 seconds by Rick Swenson. Next morning, resurrected by the opulence of bed sheets, a shower and a loo that actually flushed, I breakfasted with Rick.

'I'd like a large glass of milk,' he said to a waitress who gave every impression of having known not only Jack London but also 5,000 other gold-rushers intimately. She screwed up her eyes against the smarting irritation of her own cigarette smoke and delivered an immortal line: 'You kiddin' or somethin', all we serve here is whisky, gin or vodka.' Rick explained, unnecessarily, that Nome is not quite like other towns.

Discomfort, though, is rarely a factor in the sportswriting life. Even cricket tours of India, once rated by reporters as a four-month prison sentence without remission, are no longer the white man's burden. There are now hotels where you can get a passable dry martini though, while enjoying it, you have to cope with a conscience that reminds you that have just spent more on a single drink than many Indians earn in a month. You despair that a country of such untapped intelligence and charm can be so gutted by terminal bureaucracy and corruption. It is one of cricket's more hilarious stories that the entire profits of an Indian tour to England, allegedly lost in mysterious circumstances, later turned up in bricks and mortar in the form of a brand new house for one of the senior officials who had handled the funds.

On my first and last lengthy visit there I was surprised to be asked to close the door behind me when going to settle my not-inconsiderable bill for accommodation, meals and entertainment at a famous residential club. Eventually the secretary stopped beating around a thicket of bushes. 'I see no reason to inconvenience you by paying now,' he said. 'When you get back to England just make out your cheque and send it off to this man at this address.' The address was that of a well-known seat of English learning and what I was being asked to do was contribute to the school fees of the secretary's son. Appropriately the secretary is now dead and there is little doubt that his festering country is a better place for that.

One of the few good reasons for ever visiting India again would be to catch up with the Nawab of Pataudi, a superb Test batsman and captain in the 1960s, who hardly sustains the contention that modern sport is so grim and humourless that it has killed off the great characters and eccentrics.

Batting better than ever after losing an eye when catapulting through his own windscreen in a car crash, Pataudi returned to England as captain where his handicap eventually came to the attention of a BBC radio programme whose producer realized that it was far too important a story to entrust to a mere sports reporter. He assigned instead to conduct the interview at Lord's a young gentleman with

SNAP
CRACKLE
HIC!
RICE
KRISPIES

leather elbow-patches and an entire honours' board of academic qualifications.

The learned interviewer tapped on the dressing-room door and asked if it would be possible to speak to Mr Pataudi. The Nawab arrived. 'Tell me,' demanded the interviewer, 'do you speak English?'

'Yiss,' stuttered Pataudi, 'I spik English little. I try for you very hard make good talk. Now, pliss, enter sir.'

When the interview was broadcast next day it tended, for a few moments, to bemuse Pataudi's closest friends. The sublime Peter Sellers Hindi sounded rather unfamiliar from a man who had spent six years at Winchester, three at Oxford and whose accent, at other times, was pure Brigade of Guards.

Almost as unpopular as India on the sportswriting itinerary are the Eastern European countries. Anyone ideologically attracted to their system should prepare himself for a lifetime of hotel furniture scarred with cigarette burns, ill-cut synthetic fibre clothes, long queues for everything except ice-cream and a chilling lack of any form of humour. Their extreme efforts to dissuade Western journalists from noticing these shortcomings can occasionally be embarrassing.

Arriving at Varna, on the Black Sea coast of Bulgaria, for an Olympic Congress, I was amazed to be shown to a hotel room quite up to Trust House Forte standards. It even had a telephone, which shortly rang. 'Look,' said someone from my London news desk, 'there's quite a good story near you. Apparently hundreds of British package-deal tourists have been flung out of their hotels. They've got nowhere to go. They're sleeping on park benches and on the sands.'

A brief stroll around the town confirmed the truth of it. My fellow-countrymen, some enraged but more bewildered, looked like refugees. A firm interview with the hotel manager was clearly in order. He arrived, all smiles and urbanity.

'You are comfortable in your room?' he asked solicitously.

'Extremely,' I replied.

'I am so glad,' he said. 'We had to ask a lot of holidaymakers to leave in order to make room for all you journalists.'

Even Moscow was never as callous as that, although the contrast between the bare shelves of the food stores and the lavish supplies of caviar and imported meat and butter in the restaurants set aside for the 9,000 visiting reporters at the 1980 Olympics did spear the conscience. The Games, of course, were a massive propaganda exercise for Soviet prosperity and happiness and the lengths to which the commissars were prepared to go to promote this illusion and keep visiting journalists in a contented frame of mind went far beyond five-star food and cut-price tickets for the Bolshoi Ballet.

The most amusing, because of the subtlety of its psychology, involved the sudden arrival in Moscow of many attractive women from all over the western Soviet Union. By extraordinary coincidence if you phoned to book a table for six at one of the city's expensive tourist restaurants and spoke in English, you found on arrival a neighbouring table occupied by six English-speaking Russian ladies. If you booked in German or French then they all spoke German or French. There were mostly between 20 and 35, extremely friendly and intelligent and, despite giving the impression they had not known one another very long, were unanimously ready to engage guests at nearby tables in relaxing conversation.

Frequently, I understand, one thing led to another and quite a few journalists left Moscow's Sheremetyevo Airport with nostalgic backward glances and a much greater understanding of Russian social mores. The ladies, I must add, were all considerably more amateur than most of the Olympic athletes. Their professional counterparts had long since been rounded up and packed off to the woods.

YOUR ROOM
S NOW BEING
PREPARED, SIR.

Chapter Eleven

GOOD TIMES HAD BY ALL

On a hot March morning in 1982, wandering into the beautiful cricket ground in Port Elizabeth, South Africa, it occurred to me that it might be courteous to say hello to the local Secretary, whoever he might be. A young black man led me to an office next to the dressing-rooms where a large, affable white man extended a huge right hand and introduced himself.

'Welcome,' he said. 'I'm Tom Dean.'

Well, it's some way back to Chapter Two and still further to 1948 but there was no mistaking the man who on the County Ground, Southampton, had flattened my off-stump and with it my unwarranted dreams of a career in professional sport.

'Good God,' I heard myself saying. 'You're the man who changed my life.' Tom listened to the story and then said: 'For the better, I hope.' One had to admit that free tickets for the best seats everywhere with someone else footing the hotel and travel bills had certain compensatory factors. Driving back from our salutary reunion after thirty-four years I began to compile a mental list of what one would have missed. It was not all sport.

There were the awesome hues of an Indian Ocean sunset seen from the after-deck of the *Canberra* and the staggering pyrotechnics of the Aurora borealis viewed from an Eskimo village on the rim of the Arctic. There was the radiant goodness that shone from the astounding face of Pope John XXIII as he passed within a yard in St Peter's Square, greeting Olympic athletes and confusing entrenched agnostics. There was lunch with Segovia, patron saint not only of the guitar but of wisdom. There were the many Spanish mornings in Pamplona, waiting for the bulls to lurch round Estefeta and present them with their last chance to reverse the normal outcome of a bull-fight. There was the conversion to jazz in a night-long tour of New Orleans and

also the joining of the never-ending queue that shuffles silently forward for the privilege of staring for a few brief seconds at the waxen face of Chairman Mao, the most influential man of our times, in his very public resting place in Peking. There was the bewildering hour watching Jimmy Grippo, aged 83 and the greatest card manipulator of any age, accepting a newly shuffled pack in Las Vegas and dealing the perfect poker hand ten times out of ten. There was the halved birdie four with Gary Player at the Houghton course in Johannesburg, not to mention the nine at the next par-three. There was the trans-Atlantic flight with the charming neighbour who left it until somewhere over Newfoundland before he revealed he was Sir Robert Watson-Watt, inventor of the radar that was homing us so safely into New York. There was the impromptu cricket match with West Bromwich Albion's footballers on the lawn in front of a hotel in Shanghai, watched by 4,000 bewildered Chinese Communists, on a Sunday afternoon. In London there were the dinners, in shimmering candlelight, with Brigadier Michael Hobbs and the Grenadiers guarding the Queen. There was the chat in a B29 flying high above Texas with the man who dropped the bomb on Hiroshima. There was the friendship with the late Vincent Mulchrone, the best writer of the decade in Fleet Street, and the companionship of Ron Atkinson, now manager of Manchester United, as we roared Cambridge Lad home to a terrific victory and lots of pocket-money in a bent race at the Happy Valley race-course in Hong Kong for the simple reason that Atkinson had once managed Cambridge United. There was the ten-lap drive in a charity race round Brands Hatch which induced a fear I have never known before or since. There have been afternoons looking at the Goyas in the Prado, Madrid, and evenings listening to opera in that strange, hooded building in Sydney. There was also the morning when a Polish newspaper editor insisted I went with him to learn something about German culture and I suddenly found myself, outside Katowice, staring at the mind-rending horrors of the Auschwitz concentration camp. There have been rounds of golf in the Rocky Mountains, deep-sea fishing over the Atlantic Shelf off Bermuda, train journeys up the inside of the North Face of the Eiger and a glimpse of the peaks of both Everest and Kilimanjaro. There has been a visit down a South African gold mine, to Gandhi's ashram in Ahmadebad and to Beethoven's birthplace in Bonn. There has been money lost gambling on the pelota in Mexico City and money won at the roulette tables in Baden-Baden, home of the world's most beautiful casino. One of the most eerie experiences was simply drinking a glass of sherry at the home of the Terry family in Jerez, knowing that it had lain in the huge black cask since 1815. The only point to this list is that being condemned to write about sport instead of playing it has paid for, subsidized or provoked each experience.

There has, from to time, been some sportswatching also. It would take another two volumes to etch in the backgrounds of *why* James Hunt drove at 180 miles an hour in blinding spray outside Tokyo to win the world motor racing championship or *what* motivated Franz Klammer to hurl himself down the side of Mount Patscherkofel outside Innsbruck to win the Olympic Downhill in the greatest ski descent ever seen. This book has been about sportswriting, not sport, and it is essentially the subjective view of one pair of eyes, but those two feats, probably because of the vicariousness of the occasions, the high drama of the challenges, the beauty of the settings and the knowledge that the most fractional error could result in death, are, till now, the most thrilling spectacles I have ever been required to write about for money.

There have been many great cricket innings which could be marked for elegance or splendour but the most memorable, for me, were both by Englishmen batting against West Indies to inspire their teams back into the fight. Ted Dexter's 70 at Lord's, in the bronchial dampness and cathedral gloom of Friday 21 June 1963, was struck off 74 balls of venomous intent and was described by several who had watched fifty years' more cricket than I had as probably the greatest short innings ever played. It remains the greatest *any* innings I have ever seen, fractionally ahead in technique, though not in character, of Ken Barrington's essay in resolution in Trinidad in January 1968. Barrington's small problem, as he walked out to bat that day, was that two years earlier he had publicly declared that Charlie Griffith, of West Indies, was a cheat who wilfully threw a cricket ball instead of bowling it. Now, by force of wholly unpredictable circumstances and to a packed crowd baying for his blood, here was Barrington emerging to face a man of wrathful temperament who clearly believed he had been seriously slandered. Four times in the first nine balls he received, Barrington survived appalling injury only by hurling himself flat on the ground. The outcome of the affray was rather more dignified. Barrington scored 143 but I shall always believe the strain of it contributed to the heart attack which killed him.

So often it is the circumstance that heightens the

1st TEE

achievement. It was so for Mary Peters, determined as she was to win an Olympic gold medal in Munich not only for herself but for the beleaguered city of Belfast. It was so for Sebastian Coe, coming back from a stinging defeat in the 800 metres at the Moscow Olympics to win the 1,500 metres in a style that left so many of us that evening, crouched at typewriters in a frantic Press-room, wondering where the words would come from this time to do justice to a human being in his finest hour.

The danger lies with the wild superlatives. The fear is that you could underplay it. The object is to bring a million readers to your seat, and the rule is that when the presses roll several minutes later, your words will be beneath them. You wind a sheet of paper into the typewriter and, after such time as the deadline gave you, you reach for the telephone. It is a nervous business, every time, and when it is done you laugh again and have a drink. It is a strange way to go through life but, to Tom Dean and others, my eternal thanks.

GOOD
NIGHT